Heinlein in Dimension

HEINLEIN
IN
DIMENSION

a critical analysis

by Alexei Panshin

Introduction by James Blish

Advent:Publishers, Inc.

Chicago: 1968

For **Erwin Bettinghaus**
Damon Knight
and **Joe Hensley**

Contents

INTRODUCTION

Criticising Robert A. Heinlein, as I know from experience, can be a tricky business. On the one hand, he is so plainly the best all-around science-fiction writer of the modern (post-1926) era that taking anything but an adulatory view of his work seems to some people, not excluding a few in California, to be perilously close to lèse majesté—or if the critic is a fellow practitioner, as Mr. Panshin is, to envy. On the other, much of his major work gives the impression of being a vehicle for highly personal political and economic opinions, so that a critic who disagrees with these views may find himself reacting to the lectures rather than the fiction. A related danger is taking a firm stand on what Heinlein actually believes, for many of the apparent propaganda threads turn out to be in contradiction with one another. Under those circumstances, trying to ascribe a viewpoint to this author becomes largely a statistical exercise, and like most such, not a very rewarding one.

Given these dangers—and I have not listed all of them—the would-be critic may be tempted to take refuge in nothing but plot summaries, or in that commonest of all critical parlor games, influence-detecting. Almost all of what passes for criticism in science fiction falls under one of these two heads. By one current count, at least, there have been up to now no more than six books which do not.

Mr. Panshin, steering with great success among all these Wandering Rocks, has now added a seventh. As Damon Knight once said of one of the other six, it is a job I doubted was possible of accomplishment at all, let alone as successfully as it is done in the pages which follow. Mr. Panshin knows the mechanics of story construction; he has an ear for the language; he knows the difference between a colorful character and a funny hat, and between an influence and a common coin; he has read widely outside the science-fiction field; he has considerable sympathy for what he takes to be the aims of his author, and knows how to weigh them against his accomplishments; he writes well himself, and he has had the patience to run down and read virtually every word his subject has ever written. Every one of these attributes is a prerequisite of successful criticism, but in science fiction only the last has usually been much respected.

This is not to say that I agree with every judgment he has made—that would be expecting a miracle. But I am not going to cite any of my disagreements here. This is Mr. Panshin's book and my opinions have no place in it. What counts is that the combination of labor, knowledge and insight he displays forces one to listen to him with respect. This would be an impressive achievement by itself; it is doubly impressive if one knows the extraneous difficulties under which he had to work.

Mr. Panshin labored under the additional difficulty that his author, *Deo gratia*, is not yet dead. This would not have counted for much had his subject been a writer who spent most of the latter half of his career helplessly repeating himself, as did, for example, the late Ray Cummings. Heinlein is not that kind of hairpin. He is, instead, constantly trying something new; just as one begins to suspect that his needle has finally gotten stuck, he produces something like *Stranger in a Strange Land* or *The Moon Is a Harsh Mistress*, and then the critic is forced to take another look—not only at the then-current production, but the whole body of his work in the light of this fresh revelation. This is the mark of a writer who keeps both his curiosity and his opinions alive and flexible, and it is likely to keep a critic less intrepid than Mr. Panshin in a constant state of nerves, as though he suspected that he was being followed at no very respectful distance by a chimera—or worse, that his author is laughing at him. (Mr. Heinlein's colleagues have felt like this for years.)

Nevertheless, an author of this stature deserves to be assessed during his lifetime, if only in courtesy, and on the grounds that we owe him anything we can do to recognize his accomplishment and, if possible, increase his readers' understanding of it. All one can properly require of the critic is that his study be worthy of the subject as of the time of writing, and this requirement, I think, Mr. Panshin has admirably satisfied.

Publishers are the natural enemies of writers, but in this instance I think we also owe Advent considerable thanks for issuing this work in book form, also under difficulties which must go unsung, at least by me. Following the pieces of Mr. Panshin's tightly organized argument from one obscure periodical to another, and even from one country to another, was at best annoying—and what is more important, made it more difficult than it should have been to see that the argument *was* well organized and was going someplace. This may account for some early suspicions that the work as a whole was running away with the critic (I exclude one dog-in-the-manger response to which the only proper reaction must be contempt). In book form, one can see that Mr. Panshin had it under control from the beginning.

In short, the job was well worth doing and he has done it well; and it is doubly welcome in a field where good criticism is in such perilously short supply.

James Blish

Alexandria, Va.
1967

Acknowledgments

Far too many people have given me help in the course of researching and writing this book for me to thank all of them individually. However, I would like to thank Robert Briney, Howard De Vore, Frank Dietz, Al Halevy, and Ed Wood for lending me materials; Anthony Boucher, L. Sprague de Camp and Jack Williamson for being kind enough to make suggestions; and in particular to thank George Price who lent material, made suggestions and offered welcome sympathy. Because of the help that these and other people gave me, this book is better and more accurate than it might otherwise have been. Any mistakes herein, however, are my own.

I. PRELIMINARIES

1. The Question

Science fiction is not a widely influential field, and it shows no real sign of becoming widely influential in the future. Science fiction is considered minor stuff, not major. It is writing that is sneered at, most usually by those who haven't read it, but simply know.

If science fiction is minor, and I think it probably is, it is not because it is essentially trivial, like the endless number of locked-room mysteries, not because it is bound forever to repeat a single form, like the sonnet or Greek drama, and not even because most of its practitioners are second-rate or worse, though most of them are.

Even the best science fiction is minor to the extent that most people are not prepared intellectually or emotionally to accept it. I know people myself who are intelligent and educated, but to whom the difference between a planet and a star is simply tiresome if not incomprehensible. I know many people who can, perhaps, look at tomorrow, but to whom the day after that is a frightening thing, not to be thought about. Facts and a concern with change are the stuff that science fiction is made of; science fiction that ignores facts and change can be made less frightening and more popular, but inasmuch as it is superficial, stupid, false-to-fact, timid, foolish or dull, it is minor in another and more important way, and it is certainly bad as science fiction.

This is a book about the science fiction writing of Robert Heinlein, a man who has written almost nothing but science fiction. Assuming that my estimate of the minor position of science fiction is correct, what is the sense in talking about a science fiction writer at all? The narrator of "Man Overboard," a very good story by John Collier, says of himself: "Though I may lack wealth and grace and charm, I do so in a special and superior way." Both science fiction as a field and Robert Heinlein as a writer have their deficiencies, but both have virtues that make them worth cultivating in spite of any failings.

I both write and read science fiction. For me, its attraction lies not only in its ability to prepare us for what is to come, and by this I mean the one *certain* thing—change—but in the unique opportunity it offers for placing familiar things in unfamiliar contexts and unfamiliar things in familiar contexts, thereby yielding fresh insight and perspective. The unfamiliar seen against the unfamiliar is all too apt to seem chaotic or irrelevant. The familiar seen with the familiar is ... merely familiar, the same thing seen for the thousandth time. But the familiar seen with the unfamiliar illuminates.

Ask the question seriously: what if a spaceship full of men with not a woman aboard were to return from the first human trip to the stars and find the Earth destroyed? How would they react? Ask the question seriously, as Poul Anderson has,* and you ask something about the basic elements of the human spirit.

Say that to prevent the exploitation of a newly discovered species, a man were to father a child on a female of the species, and then kill the child in order to force the courts to decide whether or not it was murder. The question is, what makes a man? As done by Vercors,† this story was quiet and effective; I don't see how the question could have been posed as effectively—or possibly even posed at all—as something other than science fiction.

Within the field of science fiction, Robert Heinlein is a major figure and has been almost from the time he began to write. In 1941, only two years after his first story was published, he was invited to

* *After Doomsday*, Ballantine Books, New York, 1962.

† *You Shall Know Them*, Little, Brown and Co., Boston, 1953.

be Guest of Honor at the Third World Science Fiction Convention, held in Denver. In L. Sprague de Camp's *Science-Fiction Handbook*, published in 1953, the eighteen leading writers of imaginative fiction at the time were asked to list the authors who had influenced their writings. Only ten authors were mentioned by more than one of the eighteen, and of these ten, Robert Heinlein was the only modern writer. In more recent years, the Hugo awards, named for Hugo Gernsback, were instituted to honor the best science fiction published each year. Four Heinlein novels have won the prize, an unmatched record.

Murray Leinster has been writing science fiction since 1919. Theodore Sturgeon has been writing meaningful science fiction for as long as Heinlein. However, no science fiction writer begins to approach Heinlein in volume, quality, popularity and influence over an equivalent period of time.

This book is a personal reaction to Heinlein's writing. I don't believe in the possibility of objective criticism. To speak of objective criticism at all implies that there are eternal standards by which literature can be judged and that these can be known and applied. Those things treated as facts in this book are, to the best of my knowledge, actually facts. Those things which are not clearly intended as facts are my own prejudiced opinions. Even though I may omit an "I think" from time to time, its existence is implied. There are no final, settled judgments in this book, unchallengeable and sacrosanct. There are only my opinions, subject to change, and justified as best I can manage.

I have a great deal of respect for Heinlein's writing and I think it deserves to be examined. Heinlein is beyond any question a writer of intelligence, skill, and depth. To a great extent, I have taken the tack that his good points are clear and go without saying, and have tried to find his weak points and deficiencies as a writer instead. This may lead to an imbalance, but it strikes me that it is better to be too harsh with someone that you admire than to be too gentle.

In this book I have tried to examine Heinlein's individual stories, the general course of his career, and the individual elements and attitudes that make his voice his own. I hope, too, that in the course of my discussion I can begin to make clear some of the reasons Heinlein could say of science fiction as he did in a lecture* given at the University of Chicago in 1957: "It is the only fictional medium capable of interpreting the changing, head-long rush of modern life." His interest in this sort of possibility goes a long way toward explaining Heinlein's writing.

2. Robert Heinlein

Before beginning the discussion of Heinlein's fiction, however, I'd like first to outline the bare facts of Heinlein's life. In truth, this is all that anyone can do since Heinlein is a man who treasures his privacy. I'm not at all certain of the relation of the private man to his writing, but for whatever perspective it lends, I think a general outline of his life should be given.

Whatever else can be said about him, it is certain that Heinlein is a paradoxical man—that is, if you can consider a political change from Roosevelt liberalism to Goldwater conservatism a paradoxical one. Heinlein is a man of considerable personal charm and a man who has chosen to write and expose his ideas publicly, and at the same time a man who shuns the public and resents discussions of his writing.

Heinlein is forcefully intelligent and strongly opinionated, and cannot stand to be disagreed with, even to the point of discarding friendships. He has also been described by friends as sincere, kind and understanding.

He is about five feet eleven inches tall, with brown hair and brown eyes. He is solidly built and carries himself with an erect, almost military bearing. He has worn a trim mustache for years and is reputedly the sort of man who would always dress for dinner, even in the jungle. Quite a while ago, L. Sprague de Camp described Heinlein as "theatrically handsome"; and if his weight is a little greater today and his hair much thinner, he is still distinguished in appearance. He speaks fluently and precisely. His voice is a strong, very even, somewhat nasal baritone with a good bit of Missouri left in it.

Heinlein was born in Butler, Missouri on July 7, 1907. Butler

* Reprinted in *The Science Fiction Novel*, by Basil Davenport *et al.*

is a small county seat about sixty-five miles south of Kansas City and Heinlein relatives remain there today. The Heinlein family is of German, Irish and French extraction and has lived in America since 1750.

Heinlein was one of seven children. When he was quite young his family moved north to Kansas City. He was educated in the Kansas City schools, and graduated from Central High School in Kansas City. After a year at the University of Missouri, Heinlein received an appointment to the U.S. Naval Academy at Annapolis. At the academy he majored in naval science and was a champion swordsman. He graduated in June 1929, standing twentieth in a class of 243, and apparently would have stood even higher except for a natural resistance to military discipline.

From 1929 until August 1934, Heinlein served on active duty in the Navy. He served as a line officer in destroyers and aircraft carriers, the latter having been recently introduced into the service. While in the Navy, Heinlein married Leslyn McDonald (whose last name coupled with his own middle name later formed the basis of his principal pseudonym, Anson MacDonald). In 1934, Heinlein retired from the Navy with the rank of lieutenant (jg) after he had developed tuberculosis.

Almost immediately, Heinlein entered UCLA to study mathematics and physics on the graduate level, but his health failed again and he dropped out of school. He then spent about a year in Colorado recuperating.

In the period from 1934 to 1939, Heinlein worked in silver mining in Colorado, sold real estate, dabbled in architecture, and worked in California politics, even running unsuccessfully for office. Some of his experiences during the period were interesting: he has written that he once failed to sell a mine he owned because the man who was to buy it was tommy-gunned before the deal was closed.

Heinlein had been a science fiction reader for a good many years. In 1939, at a time when money was particularly short for him, he saw a story contest with a prize of $50 announced in one of the science fiction magazines. Heinlein had a technical background, if no writing experience, and the thought of writing science fiction appealed to him. He wrote a story in four days, and when it was done it looked good enough to him that he decided not to send it in to the contest, but to try it at better markets. The story, "Life-Line," was taken by *Astounding Science Fiction* for $70, and Heinlein saw that as a sign and kept on writing. By the time the United States became involved in World War II, Heinlein was probably the foremost science fiction writer in terms of production and popularity.

As soon as the United States entered World War II, Heinlein stopped writing, though stories of his continued to appear through 1942. From 1942 until 1945, he worked as a civilian engineer in the Materials Laboratory of the Naval Air Material Center at the Philadelphia Navy Yard. Two other science fiction writers, L. Sprague de Camp and Isaac Asimov, also worked there, the interviews that got them their jobs being arranged by Heinlein. Heinlein has said that at first he was in charge of a high altitude laboratory in which work was later done in developing pressure suits. The bulk of Heinlein's work during the war, however, involved projects in the test and design of naval aircraft materials, parts and accessories.

After the end of the war, Heinlein returned to California where he began to write again. It was at this time that he was divorced from his first wife.

Before the war, Heinlein's writing had appeared in nothing but the science fiction pulp magazines. After the war, he developed a number of new markets: the slick magazines, the juvenile book trade, and movies and television. Healy and McComas, in the introduction to the second edition of *Adventures in Time and Space*, made the statement that Heinlein was responsible for the invention of *Tom Corbett: Space Cadet*, the strongest of the science fiction television series for children that were so common in the early 1950's—unlike *Captain Video*, the show did not rely on action portions clipped from old Western movies to fill out its time. Heinlein was also responsible for *Destination Moon*, a movie loosely based on *Rocket Ship Galileo*, one of his juvenile novels. It was a beautiful movie, almost documentary in style, with striking special effects that won it an Academy Award. Heinlein both contributed technical advice and had a hand in the screenplay. He was later involved in another movie, *Project Moonbase*, that was far less successful.

Heinlein was married for the second time in October 1948, to Virginia Gerstenfeld, a WAVE officer, test engineer, and chemist, who had also worked in the Philadelphia Navy Yard during the Second World War. Around 1950, Heinlein and his wife moved to Colorado Springs where Heinlein built a self-designed, futuristic house in the Broadmoor section. The house was small but complete, even containing a private fallout shelter. In 1966, family illness caused Heinlein to remove again to California.

In recent years, Heinlein has limited himself to writing a single book a year and has spent his time in traveling. He and his wife were in Kazakstan at the time that our U-2 plane was shot down. In 1961, Heinlein was again the Guest of Honor at a World Science Fiction Convention—the Nineteenth, held in Seattle.

In addition to his science fiction writing, Heinlein has written mysteries, and stories for teenage girls, both of these under unrevealed pen names, but this has been a minor part of his production. He has said that he finds ordinary fiction no pleasure to write compared with the fun and challenge of doing speculative fiction.

3. Heinlein's Career

Aside from his commercial success, which has been considerable, perhaps the most important fact of Heinlein's career is his professionalism. Heinlein has all three of the hallmarks of the professional: volume, consistency, and quality.

When Heinlein began to write, he had talent, energy, and a wide range of knowledge, but he was lacking all the most elementary tools of writing, from story construction to even knowing how to run a typewriter. Looking over Heinlein's early stories, it is possible to see an increasing grasp of technique.

In an interview published in the January 1963 issue of *Author and Journalist*, Heinlein gave some details of his present work habits. Perhaps the most interesting was his statement that he ordinarily only works three months in a year. Only a professional could do that and still make a living. It is partly the result of having worked steadily for twenty-five years and having an accumulation of material that continues to bring in income. More centrally, however, it is a result of Heinlein's work habits: he begins in the afternoon and continues writing until he has a minimum of four pages of final copy, no matter how long it takes him. Done day in and day out, this produces a book in three months. I hope it doesn't sound easy. It is incredibly difficult: it means working whether or not one feels like working, working whether or not one is sick, or whether company drops in, or the sink stops, or the cat has kittens. It means professional discipline.

Heinlein's professionalism is important not just in itself, or for what it reveals about Heinlein as an individual, but because it is the core of most that is good about Heinlein's writing. In view of the central importance of his professionalism to him, Heinlein's partial abandonment of it in his third period becomes particularly interesting and significant.

The course of Heinlein's writing career can be divided into three distinct periods:

1939 through 1942: This was the period of Heinlein's writing apprenticeship, and, strangely, also the period of his greatest influence as a writer. This first period is very clearly separated from Heinlein's later work by World War II.

1947 through 1958: This was the period of Heinlein's best work. Heinlein began the period in full mastery of his tools, and ended it with one of his best stories.

1959 to the present: This period has been a period of decline and of increasing alienation. I mark the point of departure with the short story " 'All You Zombies—' " in the March 1959 issue of *The Magazine of Fantasy and Science Fiction*.

The next three chapters deal in detail with each of Heinlein's periods. The chapters that follow deal with Heinlein's methods of construction, his style, and the content of his fiction.

II. THE PERIOD OF INFLUENCE

1. Heinlein's First Period

Several years ago, Lancer Books published an anthology entitled *First Flight*, which contained the first stories of a number of now prominent science fiction writers. Damon Knight, the editor of the anthology and a critic whose opinions I respect and admire, wrote in introduction of Heinlein and "Life-Line," his first story: "few writers have made more brilliant debuts." The story was published in the August 1939 issue of *Astounding Science Fiction*, a magazine known today as *Analog*. John Campbell, the editor who bought and published the story, has described it as a story of "real impact and value."

Heinlein's second story, "Misfit," followed in *Astounding* in November. In reviewing this story when it appeared in Heinlein's collection *Revolt in 2100* in 1954, the editors of *The Magazine of Fantasy and Science Fiction* called it "quite unfortunate," and other commentators have found it seriously flawed or worse.

My own opinion is that "Life-Line" isn't all that good—Knight's comment is probably more a reflection on the quality of most first stories than anything else—and that "Misfit" isn't all that bad. The two stories have a great deal in common in the way they were constructed. If they had been the only two stories Heinlein ever wrote, he wouldn't be worth discussing at all. However, for all that they are flawed, in these first stories can be seen much of Heinlein's later style, attitude, approach and materials.

"Life-Line" is still quite a readable story. In essence, this is the plot: Hugo Pinero has invented a machine that can predict the date of any man's death. Examples are given within the story—a reporter dies as predicted within minutes after being examined with the machine (a sign falls off a building and kills him as he is going to his office), and later a young couple are killed by a car, for all that Pinero attempts to prevent them from leaving to meet the death he has foreseen. The examples demonstrate the inexorable rightness of the machine's predictions. Pinero is rejected by a scientific academy which is unwilling to truly examine his claims. The public, however, uses the machine to institute or cancel life insurance policies, depending on the length of life the machine sees ahead of them. The insurance companies, suffering great losses, attempt to halt Pinero through the courts, and this failing, have him assassinated and his machine destroyed. It is found at the end that Pinero knew of his own death and apparently was able to accept it quite calmly.

There are many flaws in this story. For one thing, it is not unified. The viewpoint shifts so frequently that none of the characters, with the possible exception of Pinero himself, even begin to come close to being alive. The story rambles along through a number of scenes and then is abruptly brought to an end. A scene more or less would hardly have made any difference at all, and that is a sign of a story that is not strongly built.

The interior logic of the story is shaky, too. Why Pinero would build his machine in the first place is never explained, nor how it was built; and Pinero does not seem to realize that it is his own act of marketing his predictions that brings his death upon him. We are given a fixed, immutable future in the story, yet the logic of the story says that Pinero forces his own death by his actions. Would he still have died from some other cause at the same exact moment he predicted if he hadn't made his machine public? Perhaps so, but there is no evidence in the story that he attempts to find out. He states that his motivation in making the machine public is to make money—yet the death he knows is coming is very close as the story opens and he hardly has any time to enjoy the money that he makes. This is not explained. The machine is apparently, in one sense, a time machine—it can measure the future length of a life—but nothing is said of the possibilities of a more complete time machine.

This story, so Heinlein has said, was composed in four days. I rather suspect that Heinlein sat down, wrote it scene by scene until an ending occurred to him, and then stopped. This is not a good way of writing a story simply because unplanned stories are likely to ramble, are likely to fail to build smoothly to a climax, and are likely to have holes in them, all as "Life-Line" does. The sort of questions that I've asked above are exactly the sort that the author should ask himself at some time before the story is finished and shipped off.

On the other hand, this story is not a usual first effort. Most first stories are so thoroughly bad that they are never published anywhere. Most "first stories" are in fact the fifteenth or twentieth story the author has written—it is in these unpublished stories that the author serves his apprenticeship and learns to avoid basic mistakes.

Heinlein's story was bought, in spite of its flaws, because it is smoothly told in even competent prose, and rolls on without lag in such a convincing manner that the reader cannot bring himself to stop the onrush and protest, for example, about the over-convenience of that falling sign, or to make any other logical objections. If there is such a thing, Heinlein is a born story-teller.

The dialogue in "Life-Line" is competent and convincing, and it shows the beginnings of a Heinlein habit that usually has been very entertaining. This is the use of the well-turned phrase—folksy, pithy, and clever. Pinero says, for instance, "Is it necessary to understand the complex miracle of biological reproduction in order to observe that a hen lays eggs?" This is typical Heinlein phrasing for you. Done with restraint, it can add a touch of vivid life.

In "Life-Line," moreover, Heinlein shows a good grasp of sociological processes. His stories, from first to last, have all been more concerned with process than with any other thing. He has always been the man who likes to know how things work, and he shows it here, switching from scientific meeting to press conference, to courtroom, to consulting room, all with equal skill and believability.

"Misfit," Heinlein's second story, is about a member of a future military CCC that is given the job of converting an asteroid into an emergency rescue station set between Mars and Earth. The boy turns out to be a lightning calculator, and when a computer fails in the worst possible moment, the boy fills in. As Sam Moskowitz has pointed out, this is the first of Heinlein's juveniles. In subject matter and approach, it presages his whole series of juvenile science fiction novels.

As with "Life-Line," the story is rambling, clumsily constructed, and rife with coincidence. Its interior logic is stronger, however, and it is smoothly told and filled with convincing detail (using vacuum to dry-clean clothes; the details of a space suit, thoroughly thought out). Heinlein's ability to integrate his exposition of strange and wonderful things, even to lecture about them without dropping his story, has been one of his most prominent characteristics, and this is apparent in both these first two stories, particularly "Misfit." Heinlein's interest in the man of ability, the competent individual, is also apparent in these first two stories. It is easy to see how closely the three Heinlein hallmarks I have just mentioned—the story of a process, the tendency to lecture about details, and the choice of characters able to do—are related. I would call it an engineering outlook.

Heinlein's first period begins with "Life-Line" in the August 1939 *Astounding*, and ends with the story "The Unpleasant Profession of Jonathan Hoag," published under the name John Riverside in the October 1942 issue of *Unknown Worlds*, the fantasy companion of *Astounding* that died in the World War II paper shortage. In this time, he published twenty-eight science fiction and fantasy stories, about a quarter of which were novels. The first of the stories were, like "Life-Line" and "Misfit," not well constructed. The last were considerably better.

There is a bit of information that I have heard enough times in enough different places that I begin to suspect that there is some truth to it. It is that newspapers prefer to hire reporters who haven't been turned out by journalism schools. The reason given is that while journalism schools do a perfectly competent job of teaching what newspapers look like and how news stories are put together, that is all they teach, and these mechanical things are the least important part of being a reporter. Newspapers, so the story goes, prefer to take people who already know something and teach them how to report.

Similarly, Robert Heinlein's stories had content from the beginning. What he lacked was the formal knowhow to tell them most effectively. A look at "Life-Line" or *"If This Goes On—,"* Heinlein's first novel, shows them to be thrown together any which way. They are consistently interesting, but in themselves they are poorly told stories, no more interesting today than, say, "Bombardment in Reverse" by Norman L. Knight or "The Dwindling Sphere" by Willard E. Hawkins, or any other pulp story of the period. It is Heinlein's later work, particularly from his second period, that gives them interest.

The stories that Robert Heinlein was writing two and three years later—*Beyond This Horizon*, " '–We Also Walk Dogs,' " and "Waldo"—all show his gaining ability to use his materials effectively. Heinlein$_{1939}$ could not have written them. That, in simple, is half the story of Heinlein's first period.

The other, and more important half, I think, is Heinlein's influence. It is regularly taken as a given these days that Robert Heinlein has been a major influence on the science fiction field. Jack Williamson, for instance, says "the first name in contemporary science fiction"; Willy Ley says "the standard"; Judith Merril says "there are few of us writing today who do not owe much early stimulus to him."

The point I'm discussing is not popularity. Popularity has nothing to do with the influence of a writer, though it may reflect it. Influence is impact on other writers. Heinlein's impact has come directly from the work that he was doing between 1939 and 1942. Since then, Heinlein has refined his techniques, and so, in their own ways, have those touched by him, but I believe that the influence would not have been greatly different if Heinlein had not written another word from 1942 to the present.

I think I can stand as a fairly typical example of a writer influenced by Heinlein. I have consciously tried to copy his narrative pace, wide range of materials, and thoroughly worked-out backgrounds, and most particularly his ability to inject detail into his stories without making them tedious. This one thing is above all necessary in science fiction—where everything is strange and new, readers have to be given their bearings—and at the same time very difficult.

These things in which I have been influenced by Heinlein are the same ones in which most present writers have been influenced. It is a tribute to Heinlein's ability that there is no obvious person who has gone beyond him in his own line.

The influence and copying I am talking about are not an attempt to duplicate Heinlein's tone, his phrasing, his situations, his plots or his attitude. They are not an attempt to sound like Heinlein (which could be most easily done, I think, by copying his folksy, metaphorical dialogue). They are, actually, the adoption of a superior technique for writing readable and solidly-constructed science fiction in the same manner that newly invented techniques have been adopted in recent years in swimming, shell racing and shot putting. If a better way is found, it is naturally seized upon. Heinlein has introduced a number of ideas into science fiction, but the importance of this is comparatively minor since only so many changes can be rung on any one idea, while the range of use of a narrative technique is a good deal greater.

Heinlein's imitable qualities were evident, I would guess, by the time he had published half a dozen stories, and certainly by the time he stopped writing to work during the war. Alva Rogers has a tendency to overstate in *A Requiem for Astounding*, but I can't argue with him when he says that Heinlein in his first two years changed the face of science fiction. His narrative technique eliminated a lot of stodgy writing, and this faster, smoother writing coupled with Heinlein's wide range of interests meant a new sophistication that spread quickly through science fiction writing.

For an analogy, you might imagine a rookie pitcher who has invented the curve ball. He can't throw anything else at first, but he does have that curve. Other pitchers learn it from him, but none of them can throw it quite as well as he can. After a few years, the rookie picks up all the conventional pitches and from then on dominates the league. That was the situation at the end of Heinlein's first period.

2. 1940

Heinlein had seven stories published in 1940, including his first novel. "Requiem," his third story, appeared in the January 1940 issue of *Astounding*. In common with his first two stories, the central character is a man of more than common strength and ability. He is D. D. Harriman, the financier who made the first trip to the moon possible, and aimed all along to go there himself. He goes at last in this story, knowing as he does that the trip will almost certainly kill him. "Requiem" takes on extra interest because ten years later in "The Man Who Sold the Moon" Heinlein wrote an account of the process by which Harriman had made that first trip to the moon possible.

In several cases, *Starship Troopers* and *Farnham's Freehold*, for instance, the versions of Heinlein's novels that have appeared in serialization have been severely cut. The book versions have been closer to Heinlein's intention. Since it makes no sense to discuss an author in terms of the fragments that an editor is willing to print when we have something more complete, by and large when I talk about Heinlein's novels, I will discuss the book rather than the magazine version.

However, the novels from Heinlein's first period were handled in a very different manner. In these cases, what was originally published in the magazines was once considered complete in itself. It was only after the war that Heinlein rewrote these stories for book publication, giving his afterthoughts, as it were. With a story like this it seems to me that both original and revised versions are interesti and worth discussing. I want to make a comparison of this sort with Heinlein's first novel, *"If This Goes On—,"* published originally in *Astounding* in February and March 1940.

In his contribution to the symposium *Of Worlds Beyond*, published in 1947, Heinlein said that he knew of three general patterns for stories that were people centered: 1) boy-meets-girl, 2) The Little Tailor (that is, the man who succeeds against great odds, or its converse, the great man brought low), and 3) the-man-who-learns-better. *"If This Goes On—"* manages to be all three of these at once, but it is mainly the story of a man who learns better.

John Lyle, the narrator, is a legate (read "lieutenant") in the U.S. Army of the next century, serving in the personal guard of the Prophet Incarnate, head of a religious/military dictatorship that rules the United States. Lyle falls in love with the wrong woman, one of the Prophet's handmaidens, who are known as Virgins. (In the magazine version they probably deserve the name; in the book they don't. In fact, in the book it is young Sister Judith's approaching loss of virginity that prompts Lyle's opposition to the Prophet.) Because of the complications arising from this, Lyle joins an underground movement called the Cabal, opposed to the government. He is found out, put to torture, and then helped to escape. Lyle manages to make his way to the headquarters of the Cabal (located in a gigantic and unknown cave in southern Arizona), and takes part in the revolution that throws the Prophet out.

There are two ways of narrating stories, generally speaking. The first person is natural, easy to write, and convincing. Its disadvantages are that the survival of the narrator to tell the tale is assured, thereby compromising the suspense of the story somewhat; the "I" of one story by an author is likely to sound like the "I" of his next; and, most important, the scope of the story is limited to exactly what the narrator knows or thinks, and that may be a very small range indeed. The third-person narrative takes much more skill to handle and is less limited. Its main disadvantage, particularly for the beginning writer, is simply that it does take more skill to handle, exactly what the beginner is lacking.

It seems to be some sort of accepted notion that beginning writers do tend to use the first person, and writing manuals discourage it. However, I suspect that the notion is wrong. I think it is simply more likely that a beginning writer will sell his first-person stories and not his third-person stories. Heinlein's first three stories were not told in the first person, but he chose to use it when he came to write his first extended story. Damon Knight once drew an analogy for me between learning to write and learning to ride a bicycle. These days, they have bicycles for beginners to learn on that are almost impossible to tip over. You might say, to adapt Knight's analogy, that for his first long ride Heinlein used a learner bicycle.

What I've told of the story so far may make it seem very romantic, and it is, particularly in the magazine version. I think this is because in spite of many interesting and well-imagined touches, most of the basic situations are both melodramatic and innocent. The book version is nearly twice as long as the original and most of the additions are simply a matter of fleshing out the story to make it less innocent and to tone down some of the melodrama. The matter of the Virgins referred to above is one example.

In the magazine version, John Lyle sees Sister Judith for exactly ten minutes on one single occasion before he decides true love has struck. The next time they meet they fall into each other's arms. (Then, less than halfway through the story, Judith is mislaid until she turns up again in the very last paragraph.)

In the book, this is recognized as romantic. John Lyle sees her twice, not once, before they decide they are in love, thus making the affair a little less sudden. When Lyle in the magazine says, "Tell her I am hers to command!"—exclamation point and all—Lyle in the book adds, "It seems flamboyant in recollection." In the book, when Judith is smuggled away to safety, it is in disguise as a load of gum boots, and when she is in safety in Mexico and separated from Lyle, sweet thing that she is—sexual and brainless—she finds another man and sends Lyle the standard letter saying so. The love affair is handled in a far more objective and reasonable manner.

As another example, in the early version of the story, Lyle, a lieutenant taking part in the final battle, sees that the commanding general is wounded and out of action, arbitrarily decides the officer next in command is too rigid to make the proper decisions, and usurps command. He makes what he thinks are the proper decisions, and then and only then turns command over. In the book, Lyle is a colonel at the time of the final battle and the over-rigidity of the next-in-command has been quite amply demonstrated.

In both versions, Lyle is shatteringly naive, but the additional material in the book makes his naiveté more believable, and puts it to good story use rather than just letting it be there as a great lump of indigestible material.

The story, for all the additions, remains melodramatic since the melodrama is too firmly imbedded in the story to be removed. I suspect this is a result of make-it-up-as-you-go-along plotting. I can't see any other reason for the coincidences and improbabilities of plot that exist all through the story. Both here and in "Misfit," Heinlein has important characters who appear several times in central contexts 'fore having nar   .ung on Tiem—a sure sign of spear carriers who have been promoted to more important roles, and plotting-while-writing. In othe words, until he got there, Heinlein had no clear idea that he was going to use these people for the purposes he did. In the longer version, Heinlein had his plot turns all set out before him when he started, so he could spend his time tying threads left dangling his first time through, something he was only partly successful in doing.

With all the criticism I have made, it is possible to overlook the fact that *"If This Goes On—"* is interesting, even exciting, and thoroughly entertaining. The story moves, it is about important things—particularly the winning of liberty—and it contains some very interesting notions. It also reflects again Heinlein's continuing interest in how things are made—power structures, revolutions, social situations, and machines.

In May, Heinlein's first story outside *Astounding* was published. It was entitled ' 'Let There Be Light' "—Heinlein has always been reasonably fond of quotations used as titles—and was by "Lyle Monroe," a pseudonym Heinlein used on those five stories he had published outside of *Astounding* and *Unknown*, the Street and Smith magazines edited by John Campbell, during his first period and on one last story published in 1947.

" 'Let There Be Light' " is the story of the invention of cold light
—light that wastes no energy by radiating heat—and the discovery
of an efficient way of using solar power. The technical thinking is
interesting and the pace of the story is exciting, but again the plotting is not first-rate. Again, this is a case of starting with no more
than an end in mind and writing until that end is reached, never
mind how. I would say that most probably this story was written
in 1939 and kicked around a number of markets before finding a
buyer, and this may explain why it is no advance on the stories that
were published before it.

On the other hand, "The Roads Must Roll," published in
Astounding in June, is a definite improvement. The viewpoint
is again diffuse, changing fairly often in a short space, but the problem is a social/technical one—combatting a transportation strike—
rather than boy-meets-girl, Little Tailor, or man-who-learns better,
and for this sort of problem a diffuse viewpoint is no real handicap.
The same sort of thing can be said for "Blowups Happen," from the
September *Astounding*, which is concerned with psychoses in an
atomic plant. This kind of story might even be called the-problem-
as-hero, and considering Heinlein's interest in process, he might well
have been stuck doing these exclusively. Fortunately, he moved on.

"The Devil Makes the Law" was the lead novel in the September
issue of *Unknown*, the fantasy companion to *Astounding*. It was
originally entitled "Magic, Inc.," and when it appeared in book form
in 1950 was called that. The reason for the title change was that the
previous month's lead story in *Unknown* had had the word "magic"
in the title, too, and the editor felt variety was called for.

There are several ways of handling magic in a story. One is to build
a complete new world to contain it, as Jack Vance did brilliantly in
The Dying Earth. Another is to treat it as a strange element in our
own world, something foreign to be coped with. Heinlein chose a
third method, that of integration of magic with our own familiar
world. In this treatment, sorcerers become licensed, and members
of the Rotary Club, and magic becomes just another element of the
economy.

"Magic, Inc." is a professional piece of work—high quality yard goods. Though the characters are well-enough drawn, the process of dealing with magic in business and politics is central here. The story is probably the most entertaining of Heinlein's first year, but it is no deeper than P. G. Wodehouse.

"Coventry," in *Astounding* in July, is, by contrast, probably Heinlein's most important story from his first year of writing. It is directly connected with *"If This Goes On—,"* picking up the United States just about twenty-five years after the revolution that concludes the earlier story.

The aim of the revolution was to provide a truly free society. To that end, a society-wide hands-off treaty called "The Covenant" has been drawn up. Those people who can't abide a free society are literally sent to Coventry—in this case, a great enclosed reservation—to work things out for themselves. "Coventry" tells how a romantic, hyper-libertarian, rugged individualist chooses exile rather than mental treatment, and then slowly comes to realize his dependence on society.

The only fault of the story is that this individual's story is interwoven with a melodramatic bit of counter-revolution and this obscures the main point sufficiently that when the counter-revolution is shown not to be quite the threat we were led to believe that it was, and we do at last clearly see the main point, there is some feeling of let-down. Without the melodrama the story would have been stronger, but even so it remains a good piece of work.

"Coventry" is interesting not just for itself, or because its point is the strongest that Heinlein had yet written on, but because the issue of liberty and libertarianism is one that Heinlein has returned to again and again through his years of writing. In Chapter Seven there is a discussion of the evolution of Heinlein's thinking on the point.

3. 1941

John W. Campbell, Jr. became editor of *Astounding* in September 1937 and still edits it today under its present title, *Analog*. Whatever else may be said about this strange, overwhelming man, whenever he has cared to put his considerable energies into his editing—something he has never done consistently—there have been few editors to equal him. Perhaps his most successful period was in his first years as editor. He found new writers—Heinlein, Asimov, de Camp, and Sturgeon—guided them, and with their aid presented a new, more scientific, more adult science fiction. Most often, up until then, scientific science fiction had been plain dull and adventure science fiction had been childish. Campbell pushed for a higher standard. How much any editor is responsible for the work of his writers is always open to question. What is unquestionable is that Campbell did offer an opportunity to his writers and did buy good work when he saw it. That in itself is considerable to take credit for.

Astounding developed immensely from the time that Campbell became editor until the advent of World War II, which took away most of his best writers. This period is now looked back on by fond science fiction fans as a Golden Age. You can tell it was a Golden Age—many of the stories of the period are still readable.

This period coincided with Heinlein's finding his own stride. If 1941 was the peak of the Golden Age in *Astounding*, part of the reason may be that some twenty per cent or better of the words in *Astounding* that year were written by Robert Heinlein under three names.

I said that the stories were readable, and that is all I meant to say. In terms of the body of science fiction or the body of pulp literature as a whole, perhaps some of these have importance. In terms of literature as a whole, many of even the best suffer from bad writing and melodramatic thinking. No matter how good the ideas, no matter how well-presented they are, no matter how well-told the story is, a novel about seven men using super-science to stage a war that throws out 400,000,000 invaders, who are, of course, PanAsians—the old Yellow Peril again—is bound to suffer simply because its issues are oversimplified to an incredible degree. It is easy to read a story like this but very hard to take it seriously.

The example just given is an actual novel, *Sixth Column*, serialized in the January, February, and March 1941 issues of *Astounding*. The author was given as "Anson MacDonald," but the name was a Heinlein pseudonym. All of Heinlein's stories in *Astounding* up to this point had been fitted into a common pattern of "Future History." He apparently felt—for the usual wrong reasons—that he ought to reserve the Heinlein name for those stories that could be fitted into this pattern.

Using pen names for their own sake usually makes no particular sense. A writer's name and record is about all that he owns in the way of credentials, and whatever he publishes under pen names is lost opportunity to add to the name and record. I have used a pen name myself, but would not do it again.

Charting the course of Heinlein's pen names is a confusing business since he never was very consistent about it. For all that Emerson had it that "foolish consistency is the hobgoblin of little minds," there is such a thing as unfoolish consistency.

The Heinlein pen names I am aware of are Anson MacDonald, Lyle Monroe, Caleb Saunders, John Riverside and Simon York. The first name derives from his first wife's maiden name and his own middle name. The "Lyle" of Lyle Monroe was his mother's maiden name. Caleb was the first name of a good friend of Heinlein's at Annapolis, Caleb Laning, with whom he collaborated on a 1947 *Collier's* article and to whom he dedicated *Beyond This Horizon*. "Riverside" comes from Riverside, California. I have no idea where Simon York comes from—in fact, I have no idea of the stories the name was used on except that they were not science fiction.

By and large, Heinlein used his own name on Future History stories in *Astounding*, and on stories in *Unknown*. "Anson MacDonald" was used on non-Future History stories in *Astounding*. "Lyle Monroe" was used on stories that appeared outside of *Astounding* and *Unknown*.

However, the Heinlein name was used on the story " 'And He Built a Crooked House,' " originally fitted into the Future History, but not included when all the stories of the series were eventually collected. And " '–We Also Walk Dogs' " by Anson MacDonald *was* included in the Future History.

Who Anson MacDonald and Lyle Monroe actually were was not

kept a very close secret. Anson MacDonald was exposed when the upcoming story "By His Bootstraps" was announced one month as being by Heinlein, and then appeared under the MacDonald name. Lyle Monroe, that writer for second-rate magazines, was exposed in May 1941 when John Campbell printed a list of the Future History stories to date and included " 'Let There Be Light.' "

Anson MacDonald was Heinlein's pen name for non-Future History stories in *Astounding*, but in September 1941, John Campbell printed a story there by "Caleb Saunders" entitled "Elsewhere." In a letter to me, Campbell said simply that this was the name that Heinlein placed on the manuscript without explanation to him.

Heinlein also had a novel in *Unknown Worlds* (formerly *Unknown*) in 1942 under the name of John Riverside, a name that he planned to use on fantasy stories from then on, the war and the demise of *Unknown Worlds* interfering.

In the end, then, the Riverside and Saunders names were each used just once. I'm not certain of the Simon York name, but I suspect that it may have been used on the mystery stories Heinlein was writing in the 1940's.

I hope this has been even slightly clear. If it has not been, take it as further evidence that the use of numerous pen names is a dead end. In any case, Heinlein dropped his pen names after the war, which has made things much simpler.

" 'And He Built a Crooked House' "—*Astounding*, February 1941 —is a bit of mathematical foolery about the building of a house in the shape of an unfolded tesseract—a super-cube. An earthquake jolts it into its "normal" shape, and it is hide-and-seek in the fourth dimension from then on. This brings me to a point about Heinlein's writing. " 'And He Built a Crooked House' " is good fun, but it is not funny. This is true of most, if not all, Heinlein stories.

This seems to be the time for minor points, so perhaps I should mention another, a constant minor irritation noticeable in early Heinlein stories. This is his habit of achieving "realistic" dialogue by the use of contorted spellings, mental lapses, and slang. Graduate architects who are made to say things like "Huh? Wha' d'ju say?"

make my flesh crawl. This may well be a carry-over from pulp magazine conventions, and even a little of it is an intrusion and a distraction.

"Logic of Empire," in the March *Astounding*, is, like "Coventry," a pure example of the man who learns better. In this case, the man is a lawyer who doubts that there is slavery on Venus and then has his nose rubbed in the fact.

"Beyond Doubt"—*Astonishing*, April 1941—was a collaboration between Lyle Monroe and Elma Wentz. It explains the Easter Island monoliths as political caricatures in Mu. The story, Heinlein's only fictional collaboration, is tedious and trivial and of interest only to Atlantis and Lemuria fans. The collaboration, I suspect, was done as a favor, and the story has not been reprinted in any Heinlein collection.

"Solution Unsatisfactory," in the May *Astounding*, is about atomic war and is more dramatized essay than story. Heinlein had the benefit of knowing Dr. Robert Cornog, a physicist who was later part of the Manhattan Project, and who helped draw Heinlein's attention to some of the possibilities of atomic power. The story was somewhat in advance of its time, but as a work of fiction it isn't at all important.

I sometimes think that all writers have something of the solipsist about them, particularly science fiction writers. Certainly it takes a touch of strange for a man to spend his time creating his own worlds. Beyond this, however, Heinlein has always shown an interest in solipsism as a theme. This, too, is discussed at some length in Chapter Seven.

"They," Heinlein's second story in *Unknown*, published in April 1941, is about a man in an insane asylum who is either suffering from delusions of persecution or is an immortal being about whom the universe centers, his attention being distracted from this fact by a set of antagonists. The second of these turns out to be the case. This story has been a staple item for horror anthologists, but I am not at all sure why. The situation is an uncomfortable one, but in an odd way it is a reassuring one at the same time. The central character has both purpose and importance, something that most of us are less than certain of, and he is in no danger of suffering physical harm. He suffers only from being distracted.

This story and " '–We Also Walk Dogs' " (*Astounding*, July) are the two most important stories in Heinlein's second year of writing. "They" is important because of its theme and because it is a good story; " '–We Also Walk Dogs' " is important because it is a very successful story. It is a story of a process rather than of people, but the story is short, the process is clearly defined, and the story was obviously plotted before it was written. Since it combines intelligent thinking, interest, meaning and plot, I think it can stand as a demonstration that Heinlein had by this time learned most of the technical skills that he was lacking when he first began to write.

The idea for the story is a good one—a business, "General Services," that will do anything, with an emphasis on an ability to find answers for difficult situations. Heinlein begins the story by showing how the company handles a standard problem—a rich, useless woman torn between a dinner party and being at the bedside of her son who has broken his leg half a continent away playing polo. Then he presents the company with a *real* problem to solve: arranging physical circumstances so that representatives of every intelligent race in the Solar System can be comfortable at a conference on Earth. If this were all, the story would be trivial, but the solution is given not in terms of licking the physical problem, but in terms of getting people to be willing to lick the problem, a different thing altogether.

It may sound obvious, but stories have to be judged in terms of what they are, not in terms of what we wish they might have been. A short story simply cannot be judged on the same terms as a novel. Though "Universe" and "Common Sense" (*Astounding*, May and October) are about as closely connected as two stories can be, though the second story develops from the first rather than merely ringing changes on it, though the stories have recently been published together under a common title (*Orphans of the Sky*, Putnam, 1964), they do not add up to a novel. In fact, they make a book only by courtesy of large type and wide margins; the book runs 187 pages and 45,000 words—by contrast, Heinlein's 1941 novel

Methuselah's Children, published in revised and expanded form by Gnome Press in 1958, contains close to 70,000 words in 188 pages, a much more normal length. If the two stories together made a novel, it would be an extremely weak one. Instead, what we have is one strong novelette, and another interesting but incredible one.

"Universe," the first and stronger story, was reprinted in 1951 as part of an abortive line of ten-cent paperbacks that Dell was trying to establish. The stories are about a ship to the stars that has taken the long way there. Originally the ship was meant to arrive after the people in it had lived for several generations, since at the time it was launched no method had been found for exceeding the speed of light, but the original purposes have been lost sight of, and are remembered now only as allegory.

"Common Sense" has a good deal of melodramatic hugger-mugger culminating in three men and their women leaving the giant ship and landing on a planet that conveniently happens to be close at hand. Heinlein concludes with a catalog of the bits of luck that enable them to be successful. The catalog is three pages long. This is not excusable. Life may be full of luck, but literature requires closer causal connections than life does, and a list of lucky happenings that goes on for three pages is just too much to accept. "Universe" is much better. It is simply the story of one man finding out the real nature of the ship, being disbelieved, and then demonstrating that nature to another. That is a real story. The background and even the plot of this story have been used by any number of writers since Heinlein first set it down. It is too bad that "Common Sense" was ever written—its very existence diminishes "Universe."

Methuselah's Children, serialized in *Astounding* in July, August, and September, involves a sister ship to the one in *Orphans of the Sky*. Both stories are set against the common background of the Future History. However, the crew of this particular ship is less susceptible to forgetting its purposes than the crew in *Orphans of the Sky* since all its members are extremely long-lived, are fleeing from persecution, and have the benefit of a far more efficient propulsion system whipped up in a spare moment by Andrew Jackson

Libby, the young genius from "Misfit," now grown up.

This story was originally to be called *While the Evil Days Come Not*. In his discussion of Heinlein's Future History that appeared in the May 1941 *Astounding*, John Campbell mentioned the novel under this title and said the title would probably be changed before the story was published. The tentative title stems from a quotation from Ecclesiastes used as a password on the second page of the story. The final title does seem better.

These children of Methuselah are a group of families who, starting in 1874, have been interbred to produce descendants who live up to three times as long as most people. They make the mistake of letting their presence in the population be known, and the Covenant—remember that?—is suspended for an all-out hunting season on them. The general reaction seems to be, "The rats! They won't tell us their secret. Kill!" The poor long-lived people, who have no secret, see nothing to do but run. They grab a ship that is being readied for an interstellar expedition, spend time among the stars, and then come home to find that the normal people have discovered the secret that never existed and have solved the problem of aging for everybody.

There are a number of small changes from magazine to book, mostly a matter of detail and name changes. One of these turns an important female character's name from Risling to Sperling. George Price of Advent suggests that this was done to avoid association with Rhysling, the blind singer in Heinlein's later story "The Green Hills of Earth," and this seems likely to me.

In many ways this is an important book. For one, its main theme, the problem of escaping death, is one that keeps cropping up in Heinlein stories, and for another, an amazing number of brilliant ideas are tossed out along the way. Still, for some reason, as often as I have read the story I cannot feel close to it. I suspect that the reason is that the story belongs to 100,000 people as a group, not to any individual, and I cannot identify with a nation. What happens is interesting but lacks all personal meaning.

Heinlein's last three stories of 1941 are all less worthwhile, not because they aren't entertaining, but because they aren't about anything important. Setting forth artificial problems and then inventing artificial solutions to them is not what makes science fiction worth reading.

"By His Bootstraps" (*Astounding*, October) is convincing evidence that Heinlein had mastered the art of planning his stories. It is an intricate bit of foolery involving a man's meeting himself half a dozen times along the path from Time A to Time B. It is an amusing set piece, logical and beautifully worked out.

"Elsewhere" (*Astounding*, September) also involves traveling in time. This is a mystical story in which traveling to any time or any possibility is simply a matter of thinking properly. This is a truly vapid story and I'm surprised that Heinlein wrote it, and even more surprised that John Campbell bought and printed it.

A Heinlein character once said:

> "Did you ever eat that cotton candy they sell at fairs? Well, philosophy is like that—it looks as if it were really something, and it's awful pretty, and it tastes sweet, but when you go to bite it you can't get your teeth into it, and when you try to swallow, there isn't anything there. Philosophy is word-chasing, as significant as a puppy chasing its tail."*

She might have been talking instead about these last two stories. The difference between them is that "By His Bootstraps" is tightly constructed, as intricate as a bit of musical comedy choreography, and arrives at a destination, while "Elsewhere" slops every which way and simply ends. Neither has anything to get your teeth into.

The title "Lost Legion" (*Super Science*, November) has nothing obvious to do with the story to which it is attached, which has some nice young people developing super powers under the tutelage of Ambrose Bierce. Heinlein later included it in one of his collections under the title "Lost Legacy," which is more apt. The reason for the earlier title seems to have been nothing more than editorial idiocy.

The story has much to recommend it. It is interesting and entertaining, and the people in it do things for recognizable reasons. Still, I am not satisfied for two reasons. The story conflict is given by Heinlein as being a struggle between pure good and pure evil, and

* "Lost Legacy." *Assignment in Eternity*, Fantasy Press ed., p. 140.

I can't feel comfortable with that, even in a slight bit of popular fiction. Secondly, this is a parapsychology story where the conflict is solved by parapsychology. The other side thinks evil thoughts and does evil deeds, so we blast them down mentally, as much as if to say, "Look, Ma, no hands." A story like this in which parapsychology is everything—meat, dressing, salad, and dessert—is an artificial business artificially resolved, like a snipe hunt in which the hunter comes back with a snipe in his bag.

4. 1942

There is always a lag between the time a story is written and the time it is published—this is a constant bit of uncertainty in a writer's life and a factor I suspect most readers seldom have reason to be aware of. It may take three months for a single magazine to make up its mind about a story, and five or ten magazines may see a story before it is finally bought. After a story is accepted, it may take another year for it to be published. Probably the usual minimum gap between writing and publishing is six months; the maximum, even for good stories, may be several years. But there is always a lag.

This explains why Heinlein stories were published in 1942 when he was working at the Naval Air Material Center in Philadelphia and not writing, and why no Heinlein stories were published in 1946 when he very definitely was writing. The stories published in 1942 were written earlier. (Incidentally, all of them came out under Heinlein's pen names; none were under his own name.) And all the Heinlein stories written in 1946 were published later.

In the case of " 'My Object All Sublime' " (*Future*, February 1942), I suspect that the lag was a long one. It reads as though it were one of Heinlein's very earliest efforts, and it may well be that early story of his that he says was rejected thirteen times before it was purchased.

The story involves an invisibility device explained in this manner:

> "The principle is similar to total reflection. I throw a prolate
> ellipsoid field about my body. Light strikes the screen at any point,
> runs on the surface of the field for a hundred and eighty degrees,

and departs at the antipodal point with its direction and intensity unchanged. In effect, it makes a detour around me."

This is vague enough to allow of varied interpretation, but, as given, it would seem that objects on the other side of the field would appear reversed. A friend of mine, John Myers, a student in mathematics and logic who has examined the story, suggests they would be distorted and upside down as well. But let that go.

What does the inventor do with this fabulous device? He uses it to hide himself while he stands on busy street corners and squirts synthetic skunk juice on drivers whose manners offend him. (The quotation-used-as-title is from *The Mikado*, and until I looked it up it seemed to have nothing to do with the story. It turns out that the sublime object is "to make the punishment fit the crime." Heinlein must have something against bad drivers—in *Starship Troopers*, a more recent novel, he has them flogged. Serves 'em right, too, I say.) Beyond this, the story is told in a curious mixture of the past and present tenses, with changes from one to the other within single sentences. For clear and obvious reasons the story has never been reprinted.

In passing, I might add that the story illustration is also bad, more amateurish than anything else. The artist thereafter gave up art for other pursuits, turning into an author, critic, and anthologist of note. His name is Damon Knight.

"Goldfish Bowl" appeared in *Astounding* in March. Two waterspouts capped by a cloud appear near Hawaii—water goes up one spout and down the other. These curiosities, along with ball lightning, mysterious disappearances, and a number of other strange phenomena, all turn out to be the doing of never-seen atmospheric intelligences as superior to us as we are to fish. The story is merely a statement of this situation, with the supposedly ironic comparison of us to fish hammered home at the end. However no resolution of the situation is offered, and 10,000 words seem a lot to spend on a dead irony. This is more yard goods, the sort of thing that can be turned out by the ream without thinking. It's readable stuff, but no more than that.

"Pied Piper" is another never-reprinted Lyle Monroe story, this time from the March 1942 *Astonishing*, and is another candidate for the Rejected Thirteen Times Sweepstakes. The most truly astonishing thing about this issue (after a letter from one Isaac Azimov [sic]) was that it cost only ten cents. It seems almost incredible in these days when you can't even buy a comic book for that price.

"Pied Piper" takes place in an undesignated country at an undefined time. As the solution to a war, an elderly scientist kidnaps all the opposing country's children and when the chief general of his own country objects to a settlement of the war, the scientist disposes of him by shooting him off into another dimension. It is all very bland and never-neverish.

These first three stories are all lacking in significance and importance. On the other hand, Heinlein's last three stories of 1942 not only have meanings that extend beyond the solution of a trivial situation, but are all thoroughly enjoyable reading. Two of them, "Waldo" and *Beyond This Horizon*, mark a culmination to Heinlein's first period, being every bit as good as " '–We Also Walk Dogs' " and much longer and more involved, and much more significant.

Unknown, *Astounding*'s fantasy companion, published something more than forty novels and short novels in the four years of its existence, most of them still readable, and some quite excellent. Of the whole lot, "The Unpleasant Profession of Jonathan Hoag" remains one of my favorites for all that I can see that it is severely flawed. Not everybody likes it. P. Schuyler Miller considers it strictly a pot-boiler. In some ways it is, but it was also written with an amount of involvement that offsets most of its deficiencies.

Our world, in "The Unpleasant Profession of Jonathan Hoag," is explained as a piece of artwork done by a beginning student. The "canvas" originally focused on some rather unpleasant creatures known as "the Sons of the Bird," but the teacher of our student found them lacking in appeal. However, instead of painting them out, the student made the mistake of redoing them in the guise of the ordinary humans he peopled the world with. Now this piece of artwork is being judged by art critics, appreciating it from the inside as men, who will decide whether or not it is worth preserving.

This explanation comes as a denouement to the story. The story proper involves the efforts of a private detective and his wife to find out for Jonathan Hoag exactly how it is that he spends his days. He does not remember. All he knows is that from time to time he finds a disturbing brown grime under his fingernails that he is convinced is dried blood.

The Sons of the Bird, who lurk in that mysterious world behind mirrors, do not know the truth about the way the world was made. Instead they have an elaborate mythology that says they were cast down and made subordinate in some ways to human beings (who are, according to this myth, their own creations) because of pride and insufficient cruelty. They do know the grime under Hoag's fingernails for what it is—their own blood—and know Hoag for their enemy, and consequently attempt to keep Randall, the detective, from finding out for Hoag what he wishes to know.

Hoag is a schizophrenic for fair. He is one of the art critics. Part of his time is spent in dealing with the Sons of the Bird, and the rest of his time, unaware that he is anything but a man, unaware of his other activities, he spends in savoring life, in the process gathering the material for his critical other self to make its judgment.

The frame for the story is a fine one. The background is very neatly worked out. The only trouble is that the interior logic of the story is full of holes. This does not eliminate my liking for the story, but it does temper it.

In the scene that opens the story, Man-Hoag has apparently been sent by Critic-Hoag to visit a doctor named Potbury, who is one of the Sons. This is never explicitly said, but can be inferred. The purpose of this visit is to frighten the Sons of the Bird. Why it is necessary to frighten the Sons of the Bird is never explained. The person who is really frightened by the visit is Man-Hoag—he is frightened enough to consult a private detective when the doctor won't tell him what the grime under his nails is and when he cannot remember what he does with himself during the day. Since Critic-Hoag can apparently turn Man-Hoag on and off as he pleases, there is no reason for Man-Hoag to be allowed to be frightened except that it suits Heinlein's purposes to bring in Edward Randall and his wife, and he cannot do this unless Hoag is frightened enough to consult a detective.

Why is Potiphar Potbury, a Son of the Bird, also a doctor? This is not explained. More important, why do the Sons of the Bird spend their time persecuting the Randalls, who are doing them no harm, when they really ought to be out persecuting Jonathan Hoag, who *is*?

If Heinlein had bothered to spend fifty more pages in tying loose ends and developing his story further, it might have been as good as anything he has ever done. As it is, it does have several things to recommend it: the Sons of the Bird; the student, his teacher and the art critics; a very nicely developed relationship between Randall and his wife—one of the very few comfortable inter-sexual relationships Heinlein has ever described; and a nice appreciation of a number of simple pleasures. Looking back, the story itself has no reason for being—the Sons of the Bird would logically have been eliminated before the story started. The story doesn't make any sense at all from that point of view, but it does *mean* something.

Damon Knight once wrote:

> It's unhappily true that most current science fiction stories neither make sense nor mean anything; but it occurs to me that as long as we're asking, we may as well ask for what we really want—the story, now nearly extinct, which does both.*

"The Unpleasant Profession of Jonathan Hoag" does mean something—and unusually for Heinlein, its meaning is on an emotional rather than an intellectual level—but it does not make any good sense at all. I wish it did.

The distinction between fantasy and science fiction is one that is usually made by saying, "Well, you *know* what I mean," and usually we do. There are a great number of formulations of the distinction extant, but none of them has ever been generally adopted. More than that, however, we don't even have a generally accepted definition of what science fiction is before we go into comparisons of it and other things. (My favorite definition of science fiction, by the way, is

* *In Search of Wonder*, 2nd ed., p. 130.

"Science fiction means what we point to when we say it," which, of course, is a backhanded way of saying, "Well, you *know* what I mean.") What we do have is a great big mess, and the reason we have it is that we insist on slapping labels on things. Not only do we not have a generally accepted distinction between fantasy and science fiction, I doubt that we ever will.

The reason for bringing up the topic is an Anson MacDonald story entitled "Waldo" in the August 1942 issue of *Astounding*. Beyond the fact that it was originally published in a science fiction magazine, I am certain that this is a science fiction story rather than a fantasy story, but I am very far from certain that I can satisfactorily explain why.

The basic elements of "Waldo" are four: a Pennsylvania hex doctor who may be well over a hundred years old and whose magic actually works; "deKalb power receptors" that have suddenly ceased to operate properly though nothing seems to be wrong with them; a rising incidence of general myasthenia—abnormal muscular weakness and fatigue—in the population; and Waldo, an engineering genius and paranoid misanthrope afflicted by myasthenia gravis* who lives in a satellite home popularly known as "Wheelchair." Heinlein has managed to tie this all together into a fascinating whole.

The deKalbs are failing, and their proprietors, North American Power-Air Co., are worried. They can't lick the problem and are convinced that the only man who might is Waldo. However, the company once cut Waldo out of some patents that he is convinced should have been his and they are far from sure that he will do any further business with them.

Dr. Gus Grimes, Waldo's personal physician since childhood and his only friend, is worried by the rise of myasthenia in the population and is convinced that background radiation has something to do with it. He wants Waldo to take on the problem of the failing deKalbs and not only work out a solution, but find one that will necessitate cutting down the amount of general radiation.

Waldo's own problem is his sickness and his misanthropy, the misanthropy being a direct result of his sickness. His success is a

* *Encyclopedia Britannica*: "There is a progressive increase in the fatigability of the muscular system until death results from inability of the heart muscle to continue its work."

matter of over-compensation, and the more successful he is the more alienated he becomes, thus leaving him with that much more to compensate for.

Gramps Schneider, the Pennsylvania hex doctor, has no problems except that he has no particular love for machines and complicated living. He is, however, the key to the whole situation. Waldo takes on NAPA's problem, but then is unable to solve it, let alone in the manner Dr. Grimes would prefer. For all that he can tell, the machines *ought* to be working properly. Gramps Schneider, however, can fix the machines, and he is able to give Waldo the insights by which he solves the problem of the failing deKalbs, the problem of radiation and general myasthenia, and the problem of his own sickness.

Completely aside from the main problem, Heinlein has included some truly lovely conceits. The best-known of these are the machines known as "waldoes," devices for remote control manipulation. Similar machines are in commercial use today, first developed for handling radioactive material, and are generally known as waldoes after those described in the story. But this is not the only ingenious idea given. Waldo's satellite home and the behavior of Waldo's pets, a canary and a mastiff, raised from birth in free fall, are particularly well-imagined. None of this is necessary to the story, but it does add richness to it.

The reason for my original puzzlement as to how "Waldo" should be categorized—science fiction or fantasy—is the nature of the solution to the various given problems. It turns out that the deKalbs are failing because their operators are thinking negative thoughts. Gramps Schneider fixes the deKalbs by reaching for power into the "Other World." And Waldo fixes both himself and the failing deKalbs by learning to reach for power into the Other World, too.

More than this, Waldo becomes convinced that the various magical arts are all aborted sciences, abandoned before they had been made clear; that the world has been made what it is by minds thinking it so (the world *was* flat until geographers decided it was round, and the deKalbs worked because their operators thought they would); that the Other World does exist; and that he, Waldo, can make the Other World what he wants it to be, for all time, by deciding its nature and convincing everybody else of his ideas.

Throughout much of his fiction, Heinlein has injected bits of mysticism, just as he did here in "Waldo." What keeps "Waldo" and most of the others from being fantasies, it seems to me, is his approach to the mysticism. "Magic, Inc." is a fantasy because the answers are cut-and-dried. Magic does work, period. Do thus-and-such and thus-and-thus will result. In "Waldo," we only know one thing for certain: there *is* something out there, call it the "Other World" for convenience, from which power can be siphoned. All the rest is Waldo's tentative construction of the state of affairs—he may be right or he may be wrong, but we have no certain way of knowing. In part, this is Heinlein's way of saying, "There are more things in heaven and earth than are dreamt of in your philosophy," and that is a far from illegitimate thing for a science fiction story to say. In part, too, I think this derives from Heinlein's background and training. As a writer, he remains very much an engineer. His interest has always been not so much in why things work as in how they work, and as long as he exposits the "how" clearly, he is willing to leave the "why" as a tentative answer.

If the answers Heinlein were to give were not tentative, if the story said, "And this is exactly what those things in heaven and earth you haven't dreamt of are," and these answers fall outside what we think the world to be like, the story would be a fantasy. As long as the answers remain tentative, as in "Waldo," the story remains one that I can point to when I say "science fiction," even though the answers may again be ones that fall outside the bounds of what we think the world to be like.

I have an affection for unified plots, stories in which everything ties together at the end. I don't mind an intriguing question or two left for the reader to answer, but I do mind questions that arise only because the writer is a sloppy craftsman. Certainly too many science fiction stories written these days take one single mangy idea and stretch and stretch it, remaining unified out of ennui. On the other hand, I have almost as much dislike for old A. E. van Vogt stories that were so full of ideas that they leaked out the sides. Van Vogt used to have a conscious policy of introducing at least one new idea every 800 words. This gave his stories movement, but it never gave gave them unity, and it was always possible to fill a wheelbarrow with ideas proposed and then half-used and forgotten.

Many of Robert Heinlein's early stories were like this. For example, here is Alva Rogers on *Methuselah's Children*: "Full of adventure, conflict, romance, and enough casually tossed-off ideas to serve as the basis for a half-dozen other stories."* This is true, but I'm not quite as pleased with the situation as Rogers is. I wish Heinlein had written those other half-dozen stories and put his ideas to better use. I think this is one of the things he came to realize during his apprenticeship.

Beyond This Horizon (*Astounding*, April and May 1942) probably has as much of a Roman candle plot, shooting off in all directions, as Heinlein ever wrote. However, in spite of all that I have said about ununified plots, it remains one of my two favorite Heinlein stories.

The ostensible central theme of *Beyond This Horizon* concerns a young man who is the end product of four generations of genetic control concentrating on producing a man of all-around competence. The respects in which he is superior to the majority of men are intended to be eventually conserved in the whole race; the hero, Hamilton Felix, is something of a pilot project. However, he sees no reason to have children. In fact, he refuses to unless he can have it demonstrated to him what, if any, purpose there is to human existence. As one character in the book says when another objects that this is a stupid question: "He did not ask it stupidly." And he does not.

Two things cause him to change his mind. One is a revolution that he sees from the seamy side. A group of social misfits attempt to overturn society and put things the way they *ought* to be with " 'true men—supermen—sitting on top (that's themselves) and the rest of the population bred to fit requirements.' " The second thing that causes him to change his mind is an agreement by his society that it might be worthwhile to investigate philosophical problems on a scientific basis—including the possibility of survival after death, which Hamilton takes to be the one satisfactory answer to his question. (Though exactly why he does is not clear to me. The

* *A Requiem for Astounding*, p. 94.

simple survival of the soul—the knowledge that you will exist longer than you originally thought you would—does not strike me as a worthwhile purpose for existence). But this agreement to investigate does satisfy Hamilton and he becomes willing to father the children his society desires him to have.

This action covers two-thirds of the book, and several months in time, and was the logical place to stop. However, Heinlein strings his story out for another five years or so, skimmed over in perhaps 20,000 words. This covers Hamilton's marriage, his first two children, and an indication that reincarnation, whether or not the research ever demonstrates it, does exist as a fact.

I said this was the ostensible central theme, because I don't believe that this is what the story is really about. I think this is another case, rather, of a story about process. This society is fascinating, and though Hamilton is the central character if anyone is, there is a great deal of switching viewpoints to give us various views of the society in action. The society is a libertarian one: to be a first-class citizen you *must* wear a gun, and if you aren't careful about your manners, you *must* be prepared to use it. Social conventions are gone into in detail, but beyond this, Heinlein deals with two love stories, eugenics, finance, and even adds a dash of satire with a young man from 1926 found in a newly-opened "level-entropy field" who makes a living for himself by setting up leagues of professional football teams. The revolution is not the central issue in *Beyond This Horizon*—revolutions and high level double-dealing have ruined more science fiction novels than I care to count, but this is not one of them. The central issue is day-to-day living in a truly strange society. That this is so is the only reason that Heinlein could get away with writing on as long as he does after his main story line has run out. That this is so is the only reason that Heinlein could get away with writing about so many different things without having his story fall apart. Hamilton Felix is an interesting character, but it is his society that is Heinlein's hero and Hamilton is only our guide through it.

I still retain my affection for unified plots. *Beyond This Horizon* doesn't have one, but I still find it thoroughly delightful. Call it an exception.

Bibliography—Heinlein's First Period

1939

Life-Line	*Astounding Science Fiction*, Aug. 1939
Misfit	*Astounding Science Fiction*, Nov. 1939

1940

Requiem	*Astounding Science Fiction*, Jan. 1940
"If This Goes On—"	*Astounding Science Fiction*, Feb., March 1940
"Let There Be Light"	*Super Science Stories*, May 1940 (by Lyle Monroe)
The Roads Must Roll	*Astounding Science Fiction*, June 1940
Coventry	*Astounding Science Fiction*, July 1940
Blowups Happen	*Astounding Science Fiction*, Sept. 1940
The Devil Makes the Law (Magic, Inc.)	*Unknown*, Sept. 1940

1941

Sixth Column	*Astounding Science Fiction*, Jan., Feb., March 1941 (by Anson MacDonald)
"And He Built a Crooked House"	*Astounding Science Fiction*, Feb. 1941
Logic of Empire	*Astounding Science Fiction*, March 1941
Beyond Doubt	*Astonishing Stories*, April 1941 (by Lyle Monroe and Elma Wentz)
They	*Unknown*, April 1941
Solution Unsatisfactory	*Astounding Science Fiction*, May 1941 (by Anson MacDonald)
Universe	*Astounding Science Fiction*, May 1941
Methuselah's Children	*Astounding Science Fiction*, July, Aug., Sept. 1941
"—We Also Walk Dogs"	*Astounding Science Fiction*, July 1941 (by Anson MacDonald)
Elsewhere (Elsewhen)	*Astounding Science Fiction*, Sept. 1941 (by Caleb Saunders)
By His Bootstraps	*Astounding Science Fiction*, Oct. 1941 (by Anson MacDonald)
Common Sense	*Astounding Science Fiction*, Oct. 1941
Lost Legion (Lost Legacy)	*Super Science Stories*, Nov. 1941 (by Lyle Monroe)

1942

"My Object All Sublime"   *Future*, Feb. 1942 (by Lyle Monroe)
Goldfish Bowl   *Astounding Science Fiction*, March 1942
                                 (by Anson MacDonald)
Pied Piper   *Astonishing Stories*, March 1942 (by Lyle
                                 Monroe)
Beyond This Horizon   *Astounding Science Fiction*, April, May
                                 1942 (by Anson MacDonald)
Waldo   *Astounding Science Fiction*, Aug. 1942
                                 (by Anson MacDonald)
The Unpleasant Profession of   *Unknown Worlds*, Oct. 1942 (by John
    Jonathan Hoag   Riverside)

III. THE PERIOD OF SUCCESS

1. Heinlein's Second Period

It isn't at all difficult to justify calling Heinlein's second period his Period of Success. The period begins with his return to writing after the war and ends, as did his first period, with one of his better stories, in this case the juvenile novel *Have Space Suit—Will Travel*, published in 1958. These years were both economically and artistically successful for Heinlein. Of Heinlein's best stories, two, "Waldo" and *Beyond This Horizon*, belong to his first period, and five, *Red Planet*, *Starman Jones*, *The Star Beast*, *Citizen of the Galaxy*, and *Have Space Suit—Will Travel*, belong to his second. Moreover, during this second period, Heinlein was in solid control of his writing tools and nearly everything he did was first rate. It is only in his third period that his writing mannerisms have gotten out of control and some of his ideas have begun to seem compulsive: the equivalent perhaps of stiffening joints.

All five of the novels that I have named as being the best of Heinlein's second period are juveniles, or at least were published in book form as juveniles. Three of the five were published in adult magazines as adult novels prior to their book appearances. This leads to a very interesting question: is Heinlein's second period his strongest because the juveniles that he was doing then allowed him the opportunity to show off all that was best in his writing, or are these novels so uniformly good because they happened to be written at the time that Heinlein was at the height of his writing powers? I have no firm answer for this. It may not be answerable at all, any more than any other chicken-and-egg question. Nonetheless, I can't help but find it intriguing. It is possible, of course, that my estimate of these novels is completely mistaken, but we shall see about this when we come to examine the individual stories. In any case, since the period is bounded on one end by Heinlein's first juvenile for Scribner's and on the other by his last, you may, if you wish, call it his Scribner's Period.

During this middle period, Heinlein switched from an emphasis on short stories to an emphasis on novels. Until 1947, he had had no books published. He had sold twenty-eight science fiction and fantasy stories, one quarter of which might be called novels. The emphasis was clearly on short fiction. In his second period, Heinlein published twenty-two short stories and fifteen new novels, but sixteen of the short stories were published by 1950 and eleven of the novels were published after 1950, a distinct change in emphasis. The change has been even more marked in his third period which, through 1967, has seen six novels and only three short stories.

Of all the science fiction magazines, *Analog* averages the best payment, between three and four cents a word. If you consider $10,000 a year a good living, you can set up a neat little equation:

$$\$0.035X = \$10,000$$

That is to say, X number of words at 3½ cents per word equals 10,000 dollars. X turns out to be 285,714 words. This is the equivalent of four novels, or of one novel, ten novelettes, and sixteen short stories per year. *Analog*, of course, wouldn't buy that much material from any one man, and the other magazines don't pay as well, which means writing even more to make up the difference. Making a living selling science fiction to magazines is not easy. That is why so many science fiction writers turn to historical novels or pornography, or remain amateurs.

Robert Heinlein had twenty of his twenty-eight pre-war stories published in *Astounding*. After the war he must have decided that if he was going to make a living at writing and was going to write science fiction, he would have to find more profitable outlets for the work he did. That is why since 1942 Heinlein has had only three stories published in *Astounding*. One was a short novel written as a favor, and the other two were novels that were published as books as soon as their serial appearances were over.

Instead, Heinlein did find five new markets. The movies and television were two. Another was book publication for his pre-war stories. Fourth, and very important, was the juvenile book market. It is almost impossible to find five- or ten-year-old adult novels that are still in print, outside of immensely popular titles, but good juvenile novels continue to stay in print and to sell year after year. Scribner's have said that they expect the Heinlein novels they have published to stay in print for a long, long time. Heinlein's fifth new market was the slick magazines.

2. 1947

Heinlein's first post-war story was "The Green Hills of Earth" in the February 8, 1947 issue of the *Saturday Evening Post*. It is a very pretty, sentimental narrative. Rhysling, an atomic power plant "jetman" on the early spaceships, has been blinded by a defective jet. He then spends twenty years bumming around the Solar System making up songs. Finally, on a trip to Earth another jet goes haywire, the regular jetman is killed and Rhysling takes over, mends the trouble, records one last version of his most famous song, and dies from exposure to radiation.

The story begins, "This is the story of Rhysling, the Blind Singer of the Spaceways—but not the official version." I don't know why it couldn't be the official version. There are admissions that Rhysling drank, wore a dirty eyepatch, and made up filthy songs from time to time, but these strike me as the sort of failings that are made to order for the official version of a life. Very romantic.

"Space Jockey" was in the April 26 *Post*. This one is about a pilot who is having troubles with his wife because his job, piloting between the Earth satellite, Supra-New York, and a Lunar satellite, takes him away from home too much. At the end he has a new job piloting between the Lunar satellite and the Moon, and his wife will be seeing much more of him.

This is much more detailed than "The Green Hills of Earth" and much more prosaic. Both these stories are typical of the new approach Heinlein adopted for his slick stories. He invented simple problems and handled them very straightforwardly, perhaps the only approach that would have been effective for the slick magazines. Both these stories are primarily human stories rather than stories of process, and that too was something new for Heinlein, and again probably necessary for his new market.

"Columbus Was a Dope" may have been intended for the *Post*, too—it does have a very simple story line. Or it may have been an older Heinlein story left over from before the war. In any case, it was published in *Startling Stories* in May, the last story to appear under the name of Lyle Monroe, and the only Heinlein science fiction story to appear under a pseudonym after 1942. It is not a people story—it is a short, simple, beautiful gimmick. A good gimmick story is probably the easiest kind of story to sell and the kind most likely to be reprinted. It is also the shallowest and most easily forgotten.

The story itself is a bar conversation among two salesmen, the bartender, and the chief engineer of the first starship, now under construction. One of the salesmen doesn't see any point in sixty-year trips, particularly ones that are unlikely to succeed. They are unnatural. At the end, the conversation turns out to be taking place in a bar on the Moon. Simple, short, and effective.

"It's Great to Be Back" was in the *Post* in the July 26 issue, and is another people story. When their contracts are up, a young man and his wife quit their highly paid jobs on the Moon and with a sigh of relief head back to Earth again. They find, however, that Earth isn't quite the paradise they remember—they have changed, they no longer fit. At the end they are headed back to the Moon where they really do belong.

While it is true that much of what we think of as "human nature" is really a result of our own culture, I do believe that in some regards people are much the same everywhere. A story like this that asks the question, "Where is home?" is going to be intelligible to almost every man. This is a good and valid story.

I know of four good stories that ask the question, "What is a man?" One is "Conditionally Human" by Walter M. Miller, Jr.* One is H. Beam Piper's set of two novels, *Little Fuzzy* and *The Other Human Race*, really forming one long story and probably Piper's best work. A third is Vercors' *You Shall Know Them*. Heinlein is the author of the earliest of the four, a story called "Jerry Is a Man" that appeared in *Thrilling Wonder Stories* in October 1947.

In a future in which genetic manipulation of animals is a commonplace, a woman with a soft heart and an extremely large bank account gets an affection for a "neo-chimpanzee" worker named Jerry who has cataracts and consequently is scheduled to be turned into dog food. Jerry can't think very deeply, but he can talk, shoot craps, enjoy television, and sing off-key. The question of whether he is a man or not is finally tested in the courts, and to help us decide the question we are presented for contrast with a very intelligent and unpleasant Martian geneticist who has been acknowledged by treaty to be a "man." The answer is given clearly that Jerry is a man, indefinable as the thing may be.

It is interesting, by the way, that of the four stories on the question of humanity, three find their resolution in the courts. If such a court test is ever made, I suspect that the answer will be the same positive one that Heinlein, Piper, and Vercors arrived at, simply because to include us all, any definition of humanity *has* to be a broad one.

"Jerry Is a Man" is hardly long enough or deep enough to allow us to extract any final answers from it. For instance, if Jerry is a man, why isn't Nappy, the miniature elephant in the story who can read and write, who enjoys music and even beats time to it with his trunk? The story is, however, an entertaining, honest and serious treatment of a serious subject.

By this point, Heinlein was fully in control of the human problem story, starting from the comparative low point of "The Green Hills of Earth." Look again at "Jerry Is a Man." That is a process story.

* *Galaxy Science Fiction*, Feb. 1952.

The author's original question is "What is a man?" The story concerns the settling of this question. The people in the story are interesting to look at, but they aren't what the story is *about*. Human problem stories are attacked from another angle. They consist of taking a person who has certain characteristics and putting him into a situation at odds with his nature, then observing what happens.

"Water Is For Washing" (*Argosy*, November 1947) is an apt example of a people story. It takes a man who doesn't like water, puts him in the Imperial Valley in California, and then throws an earthquake and the whole Pacific Ocean at him. This is science fiction only by courtesy, but it does add up to a readable story.

Rocket Ship Galileo is the first and least of Heinlein's juveniles for Scribner's. Either Heinlein underestimated his audience or was misled by someone who thought he knew what juvenile books should be like. The result is a book that I would unhesitatingly give to an eleven-year-old but to no one older.

Its greatest weakness is its stock parts. There is a scientist who has invented a superior rocket drive—but nobody will listen to him. There are the three young boys who serve as his crew on the first trip to the Moon. There are mysterious prowlers, blackjackers, and saboteurs who lurk in the nighttime. There are the left-over Nazis Behind It All and the Nazi base on the Moon. (Luckily, of course, the scientist just happens to have a rifle on board his spaceship . . .)

You could call 1947 a year of marking time and preparing for new markets.

3. 1948

In 1948, Heinlein published just three short stories and one novel. The three short stories are closely related psychologically. All three use a science fictional context to put extreme stress on a main character. The stories differ in what the stress causes the characters to learn about themselves. A very influential historian, Frederick Jackson Turner, has argued that America's strength has lain primarily in the fact that it has had a constant frontier to serve as both a psychological goal and as a test. In these stories, Heinlein uses a space frontier in much the same way as a testing ground of character.

"The Black Pits of Luna" (January 10, 1948) was the last and probably the most effective of Heinlein's *Saturday Evening Post* stories. It is quite a simple story: the spoiled younger son of a family on the Moon for a business trip wanders off, and his teen-age older brother, the narrator, eventually finds him in a hole on the Lunar surface when no one else can. The reaction of the boy's family is to head back where they belong. The reaction of the narrator is to plan to come back again.

"Gentlemen, Be Seated!" (*Argosy*, May) is based on an incident from the end of "Space Jockey," the story about the pilot with wife trouble. In that story, the seal on a Lunar tunnel is mentioned as having blown. "Gentlemen, Be Seated!" takes up the plight of some men caught in the leaking tunnel. Their problem is to put a temporary seal on the leak until help reaches them, and they solve the problem by taking turns sitting on the hole. The narrator of this story reacts like the parents in "The Black Pits of Luna"—his first impulse when rescued is to head back to Des Moines.

"Ordeal in Space" (*Town and Country*, May) is a quiet story about a man who has lost his nerve in space and come back to Earth— in effect, it takes up the dropouts from the first two stories. The man regains his nerve in the process of rescuing a kitten from a thirty-fifth floor ledge, and at the end is prepared to give space another try.

Heinlein's second juvenile, *Space Cadet*, is markedly better than his first, mainly because its plot is not nearly so over-simplified. *Rocket Ship Galileo* had some nice details, but these were largely obscured by its goshwow plot. *Space Cadet*, on the other hand, is far less melodramatic and much more relaxed, and consequently is far more successful.

The story is about the training of a cadet in the "Interplanetary Patrol." (As *Rocket Ship Galileo*, in radically different form, was the basis of the movie *Destination Moon*, so the seeds of *Tom Corbett* can be seen in *Space Cadet*.) In this case, Heinlein knows his material particularly well—the training he writes about is quite clearly an analogue of the training he himself received at Annapolis.

There are a number of novels about the U.S. Naval Academy, and any comparison will show the basic similarity. If this transference were all that Heinlein was doing, he might as well not have bothered. James Blish has labeled stories of this sort "call a rabbit a smeerp" and describes the justification as, "They *look* like rabbits, but if you call them smeerps, that makes it science fiction."* However, Heinlein is doing a job of extrapolation, not merely a simple job of reporting. In other words, there is much more than a mere one-to-one correspondence.

The course of the story takes the hero, Matt Dodson, through qualification to be a cadet, training, personal doubts, and eventual self-realization, the standard pattern for a story of this sort. What is good about the book are some of the moments along the way.

One, very nicely underplayed, has Matt as an advanced cadet doing a minor detail, guiding a bunch of newly-arrived cadets, a scene we saw once before from an opposite point of view when Matt himself was newly-arrived. The difference in perspective is startling, and it is a measure of the distance he has traveled. The problems that bothered his earlier self are simply not the problems he has now. It is a compelling little scene and is a good illustration of the central point of the book—the growing of a boy into a man.

Another, near the end of the book, finds Matt and several fellow fellow cadets having to straighten out a touchy situation on Venus and get off the planet again with a sick man and a prisoner. Their success is important for the way it is received, that is, as being no more than was expected of them. Nicely done.

I would like to digress here for a moment and mention Clifford Geary, the illustrator of eight of Heinlein's novels for Scribner's, beginning with *Space Cadet*. A few of the pictures are ordinary drawings, but the bulk of them are something quite unusual and quite striking. The figures are black, and the backgrounds and detail are white, instead of just the opposite as in most pictures. This is done by what is known as "scratchboard" technique, a process in which a dark medium is laid down on a light-colored surface and then

* *The Issue at Hand*, p. 92.

blocked out and scraped away to form a picture. In Geary's hands, the result was quite odd and added an unusual flavor to the books he illustrated. It's hard to say whether they were an ornament or not, but I rather think they were.

4. 1949

In 1949, Heinlein published another handful of short stories, one of his best books, and a very odd short novel that is still considered controversial. This flurry of short stories was Heinlein's last—he has had very few shorts published since then. Science fiction, because of its strangeness, needs room for development, and Robert Heinlein's strength has always been in his ability to develop backgrounds—two reasons, perhaps, why Heinlein has never been at his most effective in the short story form. I don't propose to spend much space on Heinlein's shorts, but I do want to talk at some length about his juvenile novel *Red Planet* and his short novel "Gulf."

"Our Fair City" is a fantasy, an amiable trifle involving a corrupt city government, a crusading reporter, and a sentient whirlwind named Kitten. Judging from the tone of the story, I suspect that it was written originally for *Unknown Worlds* and only wound up in the January 1949 issue of *Weird Tales* by default.

"Nothing Ever Happens on the Moon" ran as a two-part serial in *Boys' Life* in April and May, but it is actually only about 13,000 words long. It was written directly for *Boys' Life* and has neither been reprinted in a Heinlein collection nor anthologized. The story is about a young Eagle Scout moving to Venus with his family, with a stopover on the Moon. The boy's ambition is to become the first Triple Eagle in history and he has to use every moment of his three weeks on the Moon in order to qualify as a Moon-type Eagle. He succeeds, but only after getting into trouble in company with another boy through mutual overconfidence, and then getting out again.

"Delilah and the Space-Rigger" (*Blue Book*, December) is a smoothly-written but empty little bit of nothing about women breaking into previously all-male space jobs. The ending is a foregone conclusion: Gloria wins her job.

"The Long Watch" was published in the December 1949 *American Legion Magazine*, and is long on glory. There seem to be signs in these last two stories that Heinlein was growing tired of writing simple, slick shorts and was making them more and more perfunctory. In this case, there is a grab for power by military officers stationed on the Moon, forestalled by another young officer who disobeys orders, dismantles all the bombs and destroys them, saving the Earth and getting himself killed by radioactivity in the process. The story derives from a few sentences in *Space Cadet*—which leads to some interesting conclusions as to the nature of the Future History, a subject that will be discussed in a later chapter. Probably the *American Legion Magazine* was the perfect place for this story. I have no doubt the hero of this story is the model of the American Legion image.

If *Space Cadet* was an advance over *Rocket Ship Galileo*, Heinlein's third juvenile, *Red Planet*, marked another and far greater advance. It is primarily a boy's book rather than a book for both adults and youngsters like so many of Heinlein's later "juveniles," but it is a superlatively good boy's book. It is more tightly plotted than his two earlier juvenile novels, and far more original. The Nazis of *Rocket Ship Galileo* make it seem terribly dated. *Space Cadet*, for all its virtues, is a very obvious story. *Red Planet* is neither dated nor obvious.

The backgrounds of Heinlein's earlier Scribner's books were conventional ones: middle-class boys off on a toot to the Moon, and a boy passing through a military academy. In the case of *Red Planet*, however, I think Heinlein started from an entirely different angle— first he worked out social, economic and physical conditions, and then planned a story that might arise from them. In many ways this is the most effective way of writing a science fiction story. Backgrounds are always more difficult to invent than plots. Once worked out, any detailed background can provide room for a number of plots, characters, and situations that are completely independent of each other, and any story that is set against such a detailed background automatically has a solid base. On the other hand, stories in which backgrounds are constructed to suit plot vagaries often seem makeshift and hollow.

For *Red Planet*, Heinlein began by accepting the "canals" of Dr. Percival Lowell—one of Lowell's maps is even reproduced as an end paper in the book. Heinlein then worked out a migratory pattern of life for human colonists in which, to avoid the one-hundred-below-zero Martian winter, they use ice scooters and boats to transport themselves from pole to pole and back again each year via the canals. He worked out respiratory masks and suits with which to brave the climate. He set forth the circumstances of life: Mars is under the control of an Earth-based company with whom the colonists have contracts; various projects are under way to make Mars livable, including the major one of unlocking oxygen from the Martian sands. Most important, he worked out the nature of the Martians the colonists have to deal with. All of these things are central, and antecedent to the plot of the story.

The story proper is actually composed of two interlocking lines. One is the relations of the colonists with the proprietary company. Things go awry partly because the people who control the company are back on Earth and have little conception of the actual conditions on Mars, and partly because in spite of the non-profit nature of the company, those who represent it on the spot are to a large extent merely pocket-fillers. Because of ignorance and cupidity the attempt is made to halt the regular migrations, make the colonists sit tight through the winter, and import more colonists to take advantage of the unused buildings at the other pole. The colonists learn about this before things have gone too far, rebel against the company and proclaim their independence so as not to have something similar happen again.

The other major plot line is the relations of the colonists with the native Martians. Though the colonists have been on Mars for some good while, the Martians are an enigma to them. Before things are straightened out, the Martians are about to throw all humans off the planet in reaction to the wrong-headed actions of the proprietary company. This is settled, too, but not before there seems a distinct possibility that the Martians may cut the Gordian knot—by exterminating every human on Mars.

It should be apparent that this plot is one that an adult novel could easily use. *Red Planet* is a boy's book not because it is something less than good, but because we are for the most part given strictly a boy's-eye view of the revolution, and because the same boy is the first to discover that the Martians are much more complicated creatures than had been hitherto thought.

In almost every one of Heinlein's juveniles, as in so many of his other stories, there are small seasonings of mysticism, perhaps included simply for flavor, perhaps to remind us again that there are more things in heaven and earth than can be explained by *The World Book Encyclopedia*. In *Rocket Ship Galileo* the salt is evidence of long-extinct Lunarians; in *Space Cadet* it is an intimation that the asteroids were a self-destroyed fifth planet. Mysticism, of course, can easily get out of control and ruin a story, but the only cases in which this has happened to Heinlein that I can think of are three early pieces—"Beyond Doubt," his collaborative story set in Mu, "Elsewhen" and "Lost Legacy"—and a fourth story we will come to a little later in this chapter, "The Man Who Traveled in Elephants." In all four of these stories mysticism has been not just added value for your penny, but all that the penny buys. More often, though, as in "Waldo," *Space Cadet*, *Red Planet*, or any number of others, Heinlein has let his mysticism be an added value, with much greater success. In *Red Planet*, the mysticism is the question of whether or not the Martian elders are ghosts, a notion that Heinlein expanded on considerably in his more recent novel, *Stranger in a Strange Land*.

The November 1949 issue of *Astounding* was an odd one. One year earlier, in the letter column of the November 1948 issue, a reader named Richard Hoen had written to criticize the articles and stories in the *1949* November issue. John Campbell not only printed the letter, but purely for the fun of it did his best to make the actual issue identical to the one Hoen had written about. Among the stories that had been discussed was a serial, "Gulf," by Anson MacDonald.

"Gulf" did appear in the November 1949 issue, but since Heinlein had long since given up the MacDonald pen name the story came out under his own name. It did appear as a serial, too, but only by courtesy since the story was really a short novel, comparable in length to "Waldo" and "Coventry" and "By His Bootstraps." The story marked Heinlein's first appearance in *Astounding* since 1942.

I have a very marked distaste for "Gulf." It is a superficially exciting story and a continuously interesting one and this hides somewhat its sloppy construction, but I have the feeling that it was written in a hurry in order to be included in the surprise issue and the result was that first answers were used when better ones might have been arrived at. As it is, it is shoddy not only in construction but in basic thinking. If it had been written during Heinlein's period of apprenticeship, it could be dismissed in a short paragraph along with some of his other trial efforts, but coming as it does among his mature stories, it can't be set aside quite so easily.

The gulf of the title is the narrow but distinct gap between ordinary men and a set of self-identified supermen. The supermen do none of the silly things that the comic strip character or A. E. van Vogt's creations do—they differ only in their ability to think. Heinlein makes a very good case for this and I accept his reasoning. However, I don't think he has demonstrated his case in action.

The plot is as follows: the hero, a security agent, is bringing back microfilmed plans and pictures of an ultimate weapon, "the nova effect," from the Moon. He changes his appearance and identity on the way. A bellhop approaches him and solicits him to stay at the New Age Hotel, a super-posh establishment. The agent agrees, but then minutes later catches the bellhop's hand on his wallet, and is forced to dismiss him.

Soon after, however, the agent discovers that the bellhop switched his wallet for a replica identical in cards and pictures, even down to a scratch and an inkstain. The agent assumes he has been found out and that he had better get rid of the films while he can. He mails them after disposing of several people who try to stop him, and then goes on to the New Age Hotel. He is captured there by fake policemen, knocked out, and put into a cell with a solitaire-playing helicopter salesman called "Kettle Belly" Baldwin. He and Baldwin find a way to communicate using the red cards of the two decks Baldwin is playing with. Then the agent is taken out and briefly interrogated by an evil and wealthy old woman named Mrs. Keithley. When the agent is returned to the cell, he and Baldwin conspire to escape and manage to get away without much trouble.

Once free, the agent checks in with the home office only to find that the all-important films never arrived, and that he is suspected of having sold out to the enemy. The agent flees, calls Baldwin, and is flown by one of Baldwin's men to a ranch. Baldwin turns out to be top dog in an organization of supermen, and seems to think that the agent might qualify to join. Moreover, *he* has the lost films, which he destroys.

When the agent's new training is complete, Baldwin informs him that Mrs. Keithley has obtained one of the other copies of the nova effect films, has installed the world-destroying bomb in the New Age Hotel, and has the bomb set up to be triggered from the Moon. The agent and another superman, female model, go to the Moon, are hired by Mrs. Keithley as servants, kill her, and then disarm the bomb trigger by blowing it to pieces. The agent is killed in the explosion and his companion is killed by guards. A plaque to their memory is placed on the spot.

It takes thirty-six pages and about one day in time to get the hero to the ranch. This is thoroughly exciting. It takes another thirty-six pages and about six months in time to explain the supermen and to train the hero. This is thoroughly interesting. It then takes a final four pages, and one day, to dispose of Mrs. Keithley and end the story. The excitement and interest that the story generates are enough to thoroughly entertain, but only if the story is not examined closely.

Why are films of this importance given to one single agent to carry, rather than to an armed team? Why did the agent stop over at a hotel instead of proceeding directly to his home office? Why on Earth did Mrs. Keithley's people switch his wallet, an action that merely serves to alert and alarm him, and how did they manage to make such an exact copy of it? After all that has happened to him, why does the agent not suspect that the New Age Hotel might be a trap? Why does Mrs. Keithley—who knows enough about the agent to penetrate his disguises and duplicate his wallet—swallow Baldwin as a fellow security agent, and why should she put them together in the same room?

The communication with cards is simply not credible, particularly since they are pretending to play a card game at the same time they are stacking all these red and black cards to form messages. Try to stack 104 cards, pass messages, and pretend to play a card game at the same time—two to one you drop the cards on the floor.

Why didn't the agent that our hero's bureau set to watch him after he arrived from the Moon not see the altercation with the bellhop or the two people that the hero left writhing on the pavement on his way to the post office? Why, in view of all the hero's stupidities, is he ever accepted in the organization of supermen? Why, in view of all their stupidities (Baldwin is *responsible* for the nova effect— he wanted to prove it couldn't be done), does our hero accept the organization as the supermen they claim to be?

Why is it that Mrs. Keithley's new-made bomb and the ending of our hero's training coincide so remarkably? Why is a beginner given the job of disposing of her, particularly since any slip means the end of the world? If our hero is so smart, couldn't he find a better way of solving the problem than getting himself blown up? If the organization of supermen is so good, couldn't they find a better way of solving the problem than sacrificing an agent they have just spent six months training? Unless, of course, they were simply picking the easiest way to get rid of someone who just didn't work out.

More important than these considerations of plot, however, are some of the careless notions of which Heinlein delivers himself in the course of the story. His supermen are not only good people— all of the evil people in the world are on the other side—but anything they do is justified. In a long conversation, Baldwin tells our hero who and what the supermen are. The agent says, "You chaps sound like a bunch of stinkers, Kettle Belly." Baldwin terms this "monkey talk" and says that the agent will come around after he sees how things really are. He does come around, but the supermen still sound like a bunch of megalomaniac stinkers.

Heinlein says of a girl tortured by Mrs. Keithley: "She stood, swaying and staring stupidly at her poor hands, forever damaged even for the futile purposes to which she had been capable of putting them." All his hero had done is order beer from her, but on that little evidence, he is willing to slap the label "clearly not bright" on her. The girl is defined, both by Heinlein and his hero, as stupid and futile, but she isn't shown to be. Do genuine supermen have magic marks on their foreheads by which they can be known?

The ending, too, with its deaths and its memorial plaque, is an attempt to force sentiment. I can't help asking myself if the sentiment and glory were made inevitable by the things that came before, and I can only say that they seem gratuitous.

But if all you want is excitement . . .

5. 1950

Of Heinlein's three stories about first trips to the Moon, all unconnected, two were first published in 1950. Heinlein has not been one for repeating his stories, though he has returned to a number of themes, and it is certainly legitimate to wonder when two stories on the same subject turn up in one year. However, the point of view and handling of the stories are different enough that the question of repetition doesn't really occur. If anything, these stories are complementary.

The first is "The Man Who Sold the Moon," a Future History story. The central character of "Requiem," Heinlein's third published story, was D. D. Harriman, the man who made space travel possible, whose dream was always to go to the Moon himself, but who was never able to go. This story tells how he did make space travel possible.

The other story is "Destination Moon," which was based on Heinlein's screenplay, and appeared in *Short Stories Magazine* in September 1950, just about the same time as the release of the movie.

The stories are complementary to the extent that "The Man Who Sold the Moon" is concerned with how the first trip to the Moon —actually, the first two trips—might be arranged and financed, while "Destination Moon" is concerned solely with the first trip itself. Both stories also have in common the premise that the first trip to the Moon will be made by private business rather than by a government.

"Destination Moon" hews close to the line of the movie, but it begins at a later point than the movie does, just twenty-one hours before the ship takes off. The trip is successful in that the ship does reach the Moon, but everything that can possibly go awry does go wrong and it is by no means certain at the end that the ship will successfully return to Earth. As Jim Harmon pointed out in reviewing the story in *Shangri-L'Affaires*,* most of the problems solved are handled by the commanding officer of the ship yelling at everybody else until somebody gets around to putting things right. The story is a skeleton, worth a glance but not much more.

"The Man Who Sold the Moon" is much more interesting. In many ways it is every bit as unlikely as "Destination Moon," but it is fascinating to watch old D. D. Harriman juggling, conniving, pushing, arguing and dealing to get a ship off the Earth. When somebody *wants* something that badly and is willing to do that much fighting to get it, things are bound to be interesting. At the end of "Destination Moon" it isn't clear whether or not the ship will make it back home. The problem, unfortunately, is more intellectual than emotional—the characters are so lightly sketched that it is difficult to *care* whether or not they get home. Not so with "The Man Who Sold the Moon." At the end of that story, it is shown that Harriman cannot go to the Moon—if he were to be killed, the whole project, precariously put together, would fall apart. He can't have the one thing he most wants, and unlike the ending of "Gulf," this conclusion does arise from what has gone before it. The finance of the story may be old-fashioned and the solutions of the problems of the story not always the most likely, but the story is a human one. It can be felt.

A large portion of *Farmer in the Sky* appeared as a four-part serial in *Boys' Life* under the title *Satellite Scout*. As in "Nothing Ever Happens on the Moon," Heinlein's first story for *Boys' Life*, Scouting is a major concern of the story, but in this case Scouting is not all that the story is concerned with.

* No. 68, 1964.

Heinlein seems to have a particular fondness for Ganymede: one of the young fellows in *Space Cadet* was a Ganymedean colonist, the hero of *Between Planets* was born in a ship that was on its way to Ganymede; *Farmer in the Sky* is about the settling of Ganymede. Ganymede, one of the four major satellites of Jupiter, is a moon three thousand miles in diameter with a gravity one-third Earth normal. In *Farmer in the Sky*, a heat trap that holds heat and light has been set up to give the moon a livable climate. The whole place is nothing but rock, and it has to be turned into a farming world.

The narrator of the story is Bill Lermer, a boy of about fifteen. He emigrates from an over-crowded Earth with his engineer father, and his new stepmother and stepsister. The main portions of the story are the trip to Ganymede, finding that things aren't as rosy as they had been promised, going ahead and carving out a good life anyway, living through an earthquake that knocks out the heat trap and kills two-thirds of the population, and a final side-jaunt in which traces of past inhabitants of Ganymede are found.

The novel is very impressive in many ways. Until the day that we do have an actual colony on Ganymede, I can't imagine a more likely account of what things will be like. The story is real and the technical thinking that went into it is overwhelming. On the other hand, the telling of the story is diffuse, particularly toward the end when we are given the sort of synopsis that might be found in a diary kept by a not-too-conscientious person, six months covered in a paragraph. For instance, though Bill reports a considerable interest in a girl named Gretchen who is mentioned with fair regularity, Heinlein only sets down two words ("Suit yourself") that she says in all the time Bill is involved with her. I could multiply my examples, but the point is that enough is left out and told rather than shown that I have the feeling of missing something. What we are given is good, but I wish there were more.

6. 1951

Clearly, 1951 was the watershed year in Heinlein's change of emphasis from short stories to novels. In that year, he published two novels and no short stories. In 1952, there was one short and in 1953 two more, but after that there were none until 1957. The advantages of the novel length for science fiction are plain. One is the same for all fiction: all a short story can ever be is a *bon mot*, a glimpse of a situation, a snapshot, but a novel can be the *mot juste*, the situation as it gathers, joins, and shatters, pictures that change. More important, however, is that science fiction almost always involves settings and situations that cannot be indicated with a word as can the desert, the city, the jungle, or the Pentagon, settings that have to be built carefully and demonstrated in action, something almost impossible to do in the length of a short story.

On the other hand, the novel length in science fiction is far from exclusively used, again for obvious reasons: discipline, time and risk. It takes far more discipline to spend months or even years writing one long story than it does to throw off a few magazine pieces. It also takes more time, not just in writing, but in financial return. A short story may be sold a week after it is written, and the check cashed, but a novel may not be published, even after acceptance, for six months or a year, and advances cannot be indefinitely extended. Finally, banking all on a long story that might fail is a risky business. An unsold short story is only four thousand wasted words, but a novel that isn't published or that sells poorly is a disaster. By 1951, Heinlein apparently felt he could afford to take the risk and concentrate on writing novels.

Heinlein's novels in 1951 were *The Puppet Masters*, his first adult novel since 1942, and *Between Planets*, the first of his novels for Scribner's to be serialized in an adult magazine* before book publication.

Donald Harvey, the hero of *Between Planets*, like John Lyle of *"If This Goes On—"* and Larry Smith in Heinlein's 1956 novel *Double Star*, is an apolitical fellow who gets into politics up to his neck. Lyle gets involved for the love of a fair maid, Smith for love of eating regularly. Harvey becomes involved for the most likely reason of all: he simply has no other choice.

* *Blue Book*, Sept., Oct. 1951, under the title *Planets in Combat*.

In the world of *Between Planets*, humans have colonies on both Mars and Venus. The Martians are an old and dying race, the Venerians—long-lived "dragons"—are a lively, intelligent race fully on a par with our own. Over a period of two centuries the government of Earth has been growing more repressive, both with its colonies and at home. The colony on Venus is on the point of revolt. Don Harvey could not be less involved. He was born in orbit between Luna and Ganymede, his mother a Venus national, his father a citizen of Earth. Harvey, a schoolboy of seventeen or so, has no fixed political ideas, no national allegiance.

This situation is the author's way of setting his hero up for the kill. Take a nice, fresh young boy wrapped in his own concerns and then put him in a situation where he has to worry about his liberty. If somebody treats you as an enemy and simply won't go away and leave you alone, then, whether you like it or not, you *are* involved.

That is exactly what happens to Don Harvey.

As the story opens, Harvey is in school in New Mexico. There is war in the air. Suddenly Don gets a message from his parents, distinguished scientists doing work in the small human community on Mars, telling him to drop out of school now, in the middle of the term, and come to Mars. And he is to see a Dr. Jefferson, a friend of his parents, before he comes.

Heinlein thoroughly demonstrates the repressive nature of the Earth government, thoroughly enough that when Don gets to the space station around Earth and finds that a raiding party from the Venus colony has come to blow it up, seizing his ship for Mars at the same time, he opts to head for Venus rather than back to Earth. However he is still apolitical—his interest is in getting to Mars, not in fighting for Venus. It takes a landing on Venus by Earth troops, butchery, and Don's grasping of the idea that *he* is very definitely wanted by the security police for a ring that Dr. Jefferson gave him to take to his parents for Don to definitely decide that there is a time to start fighting.

The ring turns out to be the key to the whole story. There has been an interplanetary brotherhood of scientists trying to keep information free and circulating in spite of the government. Dr. Jef-

ferson, Don's parents, and most of the people Don makes friends
with throughout the story all belong. The ring contains one-half
the information needed to end the war. The information was meant
to be assembled on Mars, but the war has caused both fragments to
wind up on Venus, except that no one has known that Don Harvey,
a last minute choice as an unknowing courier, has the information
or that he is on Venus. The information is eventually assembled and
adds up to a souped-up space drive and a force field at a minimum.
As usual, Heinlein takes an engineering attitude to this—his interest
is in what it does rather than in how it works—but at the same time
he avoids super-science doubletalk in explanation and the production
of inventions in ten minutes. In other words, he has an engineer's
respect for science. The new discoveries are enough to end the war,
since all that is necessary to bring Earth to its knees is a lid over a
few of its most important cities.

There is a certain amount of melodrama inherent in a plot like
this, but to Heinlein's credit, the melodrama only occasionally becomes overwhelming, as in lines like, "Don held the knife with the
relaxed thumb-and-two-finger grip of those who understand steel."
(I understand that everybody at US Steel holds his knife in this
manner.) The Venus setting is very well done, and so is the feeling of
an uncertain, unstable time. Again, however, as in *Farmer in the Sky*,
I have the feeling that something is missing, that after a certain point
Heinlein is simply trying to tie things together and end the story.

The Puppet Masters (*Galaxy*, September, October, November 1951)
is the most ambitious of the three specifically adult novels that Heinlein wrote between *Beyond This Horizon* in 1942 and *Stranger in a
Strange Land* in 1961. As a story it is both typical and atypical of
Heinlein. It shares with *Between Planets* the very common Heinlein
theme of preserving liberty. However, it is one of the very few Heinlein stories that are aimed at the viscera rather than at the intellect.
The liberty that Heinlein aims to preserve is freedom to use one's
own mind, and he means us to *feel* his case as well as merely
understand it.

The basic theme of *The Puppet Masters* is, I'm told, an old one.

Boucher and McComas, for instance, in reviewing *The Puppet Masters* in *The Magazine of Fantasy and Science Fiction* said:

> In *The Puppet Masters* he's chosen a theme which old-line aficio-
> nados will consider tired and even tiresome: the invasion of earth
> by interplanetary parasites who fasten upon men and convert them
> into soulless zombies.*

I can believe that this is an ancient idea—it is so compelling, so frightening, so elemental that it is bound to be—but the actual inci-dence of its appearance in modern science fiction is quite small. And Heinlein's handling of the theme, as Boucher and McComas went on to point out, is tremendously effective.

The parasites are slugs from Titan, the largest of Saturn's moons. Their vehicles are flying saucers, one of the earliest and most effective fictional uses of them that I can recall. The slugs attach themselves to the backs of humans and turn them into automatons. In abstract this is bad enough, but Heinlein has his narrator, a tough, smart, and, of course, competent security agent, ridden for a time by the slugs so that you know and feel what it is like. It is not a pleasant thing to read about.

The slugs are well on their way to taking over the country before we can begin to mobilize. The situation eventually stabilizes pre-cariously with the slugs in possession of the middle third of the United States, and probably in control of Russia. Then it is dis-covered that the slugs are susceptible to a Venerian disease that kills humans in nine days, slugs in less. Animals are inoculated with the disease and sent into the possessed areas, to infect any slug that rides them. The slugs communicate by direct contact, which involves ex-change of body material, so that soon all the slugs in the United States have the disease. Teams are then sent in with antidotes to save the humans before they, too, die. The story ends with a human ship bound for Titan to give the slugs hell.

The story makes greater emotional than logical sense. For in-stance, at one point the hero is captured by the slugs and then recaptured later by his own people. The slug on his back turns out to be the *only* one they have, though there are a good number of

* February, 1952.

slug-ridden people in the city. More important, though, is that if the titans are susceptible to disease, and disease can kill them when they exchange body material, how have they survived to this point?

One of the most chilling things in the story is the degeneration of people under the control of the slugs. They don't bathe, shave, eat, go to the bathroom, or do anything else unless the slugs let them, and much of the time the slugs don't let them. A real point is made of this: " '...a little guy called 'Jake' who was washroom attendant, but he had to be disposed of later—his master would not let him take time out for necessities.' " This seems self-defeating for the slugs. They have command of the knowledge of the people they ride—why wouldn't they pamper us as we pamper the animals that we live off? The answer, of course, is that the degeneration is meaningful as emotion and as a symbol of what happens to people who have lost their independence, something that genuinely affects Heinlein at his deepest level.

There are many similarities between *The Puppet Masters* and Heinlein's 1959 prize-winning novel, *Starship Troopers*. The nature of the enemy is much the same: implacable and sharing a common mind. The nature of the fight is the same: all-or-nothing, total defeat or total victory. And, as George Price has pointed out, the nature of the solution is the same: man is the hairiest fighting animal in this end of the universe—tackle him at your own peril. The final words of *The Puppet Masters* are, "I feel exhilarated. Puppet masters—the free men are coming to kill you! *Death and Destruction!*" Given the premises of the two stories, this is Heinlein's answer. I think *The Puppet Masters* states problem and solution better, and is definitely the more successful book.

I myself don't place this book among Heinlein's very best, though I think it is a good one and as disturbing a book as I have ever read. I can, however, see the case for anyone who wants to nominate it for one of Heinlein's best.

7. 1952

It seems to me that fiction generally has to suppose the existence of free will—if a story's end is determined before the story begins, it is hardly necessary to read it to find out what happens. That is oversimple, of course, but I do prefer stories that are about human problems solved by human beings. Anything else is more a statement of a situation than a story.

"The Year of the Jackpot," a novelette in the March 1952 *Galaxy*, is nothing but the statement of a situation. There is a human problem: everybody is acting unsanely. There is no human solution, however. The reason given for our actions is that we are caught in the grip of cycles—cycles in fashions, cycles in economics, cycles in everything. As the statistician protagonist of the story, who has been charting all of the cycles, says, we are lemmings. We can't help ourselves. The jackpot year of the title is the one in which all the good cycles are at their lowest and all of the bad ones are at their peaks. The story ends with the sun blowing up, the culmination of one final cycle.

Still, in spite of the story being no more than the statement of a situation, I do like "The Year of the Jackpot." Perhaps it is because the main characters remain interesting and attractive, for all their helplessness, right until the end.

Heinlein's novel for Scribner's in 1952 was *The Rolling Stones*, entitled *Tramp Space Ship* when it was serialized in *Boys' Life*. It may have been written directly for *Boys' Life*. Certainly its simple, uncomplicated plot is likely to appeal to boys a year or two younger than those that would enjoy *Between Planets* or some of Heinlein's other juveniles. A change in the nature of Heinlein's juvenile protagonists can be seen from his earliest books. In all those up through *The Rolling Stones*, with the exception of *Between Planets*, we have heroes who are essentially dependent on their parents or other adults. In all the books after *The Rolling Stones*, with the exception of *Podkayne of Mars* (which is not a Scribner's book and falls in a different period), we are presented with heroes who are not dependent on adults in the same way, but who make their own way in the world. An important change, it seems to me.

The Rolling Stones is constructed in the simplest manner possible. Start, and then add "ands" until the story has gone on long enough and you decide to end it. The "ands" are additional episodes. It is an uncomplicated way of telling a story, tedious if done badly, easy to enjoy if done well.

The Stones are a family. Roger, ex-mayor of Luna City, engineer, and author of the video serial *The Scourge of the Spaceways*, is the head of the family. Hazel Stone, his mother, is a fresh, lively oldster, one of the original citizens of the Moon, and an engineer herself. She takes over writing the video serial soon after the story begins. Edith Stone, Roger's wife, is a doctor and a sculptress. Their children are Lowell, four years old but able to beat Hazel at chess, use a slide rule and Lord knows what-all-else; Meade, a bright but somewhat undefined girl of something less than twenty; and Castor and Pollux, fifteen-year-old twins, inventors of a "frostproof rebreather valve" from which they have realized a considerable amount of money, budding young businessmen, general hell-raisers, and story protagonists.

The Scourge of the Spaceways and the unlimited nature of the various skills spread through the family make it financially possible for them to buy a spaceship and simply leave home on a *Wanderjahr*. The original impetus for the journey is the goading of the twins, who were in mind to do it all by themselves, but the whole family finds itself in favor. The Stones travel from the Moon to Mars, and when Mars palls they push on to the site of a mining strike in the Asteroids. At the end, they are bound on to Titan, the largest moon of Saturn. And on from there to who knows where.

As punctuation there is Heinlein's usual wealth of detail and a number of little adventures—epidemic on board another ship, jettisoning and recovering cargo, a lost space-scooter with Hazel and Lowell aboard—that are underplayed enough to seem just exactly the sort of thing that might happen to normal people like the Stones rather than to idiot-adventure heroes like the Scourge of the Spaceways.

Before I leave this story, I would like to point out one last thing that I particularly liked. Writing is not completely unlike juggling and it is difficult to do everything at once. Scenes with one or two characters are not at all hard to write, but every extra character you add and use makes the scene that much more difficult. To approach a scene with five living, breathing, thinking characters in it takes a deep breath and rolling up one's sleeves. Several times, however, in *The Rolling Stones*, including the first chapter, Heinlein has all seven members of the Stone family on stage at once, all talking, all going on at cross-purposes. I respect him for even trying it, but he brings it off beautifully.

8. 1953

"Project Nightmare" (*Amazing*, April 1953) is smoothly written, but crude. It is quite obvious that if you make the proper premises you can force almost any conclusion as "right" and "inevitable." Heinlein's premises in this story are that the military have located people with wild talents of a sophisticated order, and that the Russians try to blackmail us into capitulation by planting atomic devices in thirty-eight of our major cities. The spectacular crudeness of this story can be seen in that Russia's announcement comes on the very day that the ESPers prove that they can mentally set off atomic weapons. It turns out that they can damp them, too, and they hold the bombs from going off in thirty-seven of the thirty-eight cities until they can be located and disposed of. At the end, the ESPers are prepared to set off all of Russia's stockpiled nuclear weapons.

"Sky Lift" (*Imagination*, November 1953) is simpler but much more impressive. A small scientific community on Pluto has been struck by a degenerative blood disease and they need a blood bank. Getting it to them involves two men blasting at a constant three and one-half gravities for more than nine days. Two hundred and seventy people are saved, but the cost is one man dead and the other turned into a moron.

The issues of "Project Nightmare" are artificial ones. Those of "Sky Lift" are real, immediate and important. That is the difference between a story that means something and one that doesn't.

Starman Jones is one of Heinlein's most effective books. It shows a young man in a situation where anything he does is bound to put him in the wrong. That is a nice, difficult sort of problem, the sort that fiction really ought to be concerned with. Heinlein's solution is the most viable one that I can imagine: when all your choices are "wrong" ones, you pick the one you like best and live with its consequences.

In *Starman Jones* the Earth is crowded and jobs are at a premium. For this reason, the best jobs are held by inheritance, passed down through a restrictive guild system. If you don't like what you have inherited, presuming that you have inherited something, it takes money and trading to get something else. If you have no money and no guild job, you are just out of luck.

Max Jones is a hill boy whose uncle belonged to the Astrogators' Guild, but who died before he could nominate Max. Max wants nothing more than to serve on a starship, but without the nomination he doesn't stand a chance. Not only does the Guild deny Max the chance he thought he had in space, but it takes his uncle's books from him (the secret mathematics of the Guild which outsiders mustn't see) and gives him pennies in compensation. With the only other alternative to return home to a fatuous stepmother and her new husband, a thorough-going scoundrel, Max joins a dubious acquaintance and with the aid of false papers the two sneak their way into menial starship jobs, Max figuring this is better than nothing.

Max has going for him the fact that his uncle was known and respected, and his own mathematical ability and photographic memory. He knows those "secret" mathematical tables, and he has the brains to learn how to use them. Against him is the fact that eventually he will be found out. He plans to jump ship before it returns to Earth, but some of his uncle's old associates and a notation on his phony records that he has once struck for the job of chartsman—a starplotter in the control room—get him another shot at the job. His demonstrated abilities earn him a try at the job of astrogator, exactly what he has always wanted—in spite of the restrictions of the Guild there are hardly enough people around with the requisite abilities to fill the jobs open. (That, by the way, causes me to wonder if astrogators' jobs would ever be handed around by a guild system. Plumb-

ing and trucking jobs, yes, but jobs involving advanced mathematics?)
In any case, a death, a senile breakdown, and a case of paranoia leave
Max with the job of bringing the ship home when she gets lost. The
consequences that Max has to live with are a reprimand and a stiff
fine, but at the end he is ready to ship out again as an astrogator.

Starman Jones demonstrates the advantages in having an older protagonist. First, the world he can move in is much wider, and second,
a Max Jones bringing the ship home is credible while a Pollux Stone
bringing the ship home would not be. This is a long book, over 300
pages, and a rich one. It is a solid, detailed, fascinating piece of work.

9. 1954

This brings me to the question of just what a juvenile novel is,
anyway. As our publishing industry is run, in most cases there isn't
much question. *Freddy the Pig* is on one side of the line and *Lolita*
is on the other, sharply distinct.

However, there are plenty of so-called "adult" books that are of
legitimate interest to children, and any good children's book will
very likely be read by adults as well. Is *Charlotte's Web* just a
children's book? *Moby Dick* and *Huckleberry Finn*, counted the
two best American novels, are read by children. It seems to me that
any book published for children that adults cannot enjoy is likely to
be a pretty poor book. And if some adult books cannot be enjoyed
or understood by children, there are plenty of adults who cannot
enjoy or understand them either. I don't see any distinct line and I
doubt that there is one. As it is now, a juvenile book is a book that
the publishing industry packages and sells as a juvenile.

The Star Beast, Heinlein's "juvenile" novel for 1954, is a good
illustration. It was serialized as an adult novel in *The Magazine of
Fantasy and Science Fiction* (May, June, July 1954) and then published by Scribner's as a juvenile novel and marketed in a juvenile
package with a simple-minded blurb that begins, "Robert Heinlein's
'space zoo' is unique—there is an unusual animal in each of his
books"—untrue, by the way, of even his books for Scribner's.
Either Scribner's has a much higher opinion of the minds of children

than most publishers—a notion belied by their jacket blurbs—or they were so used to publishing Heinlein's books as juveniles that they never stopped to think twice. A third alternative doesn't occur to me. Perhaps it is Heinlein's fault for writing a book that can be interesting to almost any age.

The Star Beast is really about a diplomatic incident, not about unusual animals from outer space. There are two main story lines. A ship has appeared in our skies claiming that we are holding prisoner one of their own, a party to a six-sex marriage that has been planned for two thousand years, part of a larger genetic schema that has been under way for thirty-eight thousand years. The other line follows the trouble gotten into by Lummox, the pet of John Thomas Stuart XI.

Lummox is an extraterrestrial brought home by John Thomas's great-grandfather, a crew member on one of the earliest interstellar ships of exploration. Lummox loves steel (he once ate a second-hand Buick) and is the size of half a house (either half). He has the right number of legs—eight—to be the missing Hroshia, but his size and lack of arms seem to rule him out, so when he inadvertently causes a considerable amount of damage, starting with a dog and some rose bushes and ending with part of a department store, he is scheduled to be done away with. It turns out, however, that Lummox is a "she," the missing heiress, and also that the Hroshii may well be capable of destroying Earth if they are frustrated in getting her back. It is then up to the Department of Spatial Affairs and its Permanent Under Secretary, Henry Kiku, to straighten things out.

Of Kiku, Damon Knight says:

> It's a pure delight to watch him at work. Heinlein's interest, as always, is in The Man Who Knows How, other types appearing only as caricatures, and if this makes for a distorted view of humanity, it also makes for close-textured, fascinating writing. Stories about know-nothings inevitably repeat the same stock motions; the repertory of competence is inexhaustible.*

The dealings of Kiku, his understudy Sergei Greenberg, and Dr. Ftaeml, the medusa humanoid go-between for the Hroshii, are

---

* *In Search of Wonder*, 2nd ed., p. 83.

nothing short of fascinating. Only a little more than half of the book is directly concerned with John Thomas and Lummox, the rest is Kiku's show and he makes the most of it.

Besides the usual Heinlein touches (the double for the Secretary General of the Federation who sits through dull formal programs, for instance, a notion that later grew into an entire book of its own in *Double Star*), this book stands by itself among Heinlein's books in being filled with satire and black humor:

John Thomas's girl friend, Betty Sorenson, lives in the Westville Home for Free Children: she has divorced her parents for their odd ideas.

Mr. Kiku's stomach can't stand snakes, so every time he meets Dr. Ftaeml, whose head writhes with tendrils, it is an ordeal for him.

As Damon Knight said, most of the characters in this book are caricatures, as, of course, is likely to be true in any satirical book. The culmination is probably Mrs. Beulah Murgatroyd, inventor of the popular puppet Pidgie-Widgie (*Pidgie-Widgie on the Moon*, *Pidgie-Widgie Goes to Mars*, *Pidgie-Widgie and the Space Pirates*) and the power behind "The Friends of Lummox." Mrs. Murgatroyd earnestly desires Mr. Kiku to come on stereovision with her and Pidgie-Widgie and talk things over while they all settle down to a nice bowl of Hunkies. Heinlein must have been pleased with that one, and with

> ...the terrible, hushed-up occasion when a member of the official family of the Ambassador from Llador had been found, dead and stuffed, in a curiosity shop in the Virgin Islands.

And finally, Lummox's view of the matter is that she has been spending a hundred years in raising John Thomases, and she damned well plans to continue. She won't go home unless she has her way, and so, when she goes, John Thomas and Betty go with her. Luck, Lummox.

10. 1955

As I say, I don't understand the juvenile publishing industry. *Starman Jones*, *The Star Beast*, and Heinlein's Scribner's novel for 1955, *Tunnel in the Sky*, all share a darkness in tone that you just don't expect in children's books. It may be that there is a tremendous hunger for bleak children's books and the manuscripts just cannot be found.

The blackness of *Starman Jones* lies in the society portrayed. The blackness of *The Star Beast* lies in its attitude. These are both very successful books. *Tunnel in the Sky* is less successful, partly because Heinlein gets tired about two-thirds of the way through and rushes his ending. This seems to happen in those Heinlein stories in which the action is spread over a number of years. In a moment I will come to the other reason for *Tunnel in the Sky*'s lack of complete realization.

The basic idea for the story is one of the best ever invented, elemental enough to stand a thousand usings. In essence, it is to strip a character of everything but a toothpick and a piece of chicken wire and chuck him out into a hostile wilderness. In a Murray Leinster story he turns the toothpick and the chicken wire into a blaster and a spaceship (with the aid of a little bit of native ingenuity) and hops off to conquer the universe. In a Robert Heinlein story, with the aid of his native ingenuity, the character survives.

In this case, the hero is Rod Walker, a high school senior enrolled in Advanced Survival, Course 410. The members of the class get their choice of weapons and are then dropped: "(a) ANY planet, ANY climate, ANY terrain; (b) NO rules, ALL weapons, ANY equipment." With skill and luck, they survive.

The "Ramsbotham Gate"—step through on this side and step out somewhere else—has made thousands of planets available to Earth, but most of them have their own particular dangers. Trained men are needed to cope with them, and courses like the one that Walker takes are given both at high school and college level to train them as much as possible.

Walker's group is dropped for a period of two to ten days, but the pickup is never made. They and other classes dropped on this who-knows-where have to band together and make something of themselves. After two years contact is re-established—a supernova in the immediate stellar vicinity threw all calculations off and finding the kids again has been a hit-or-miss operation. The beauty of the story is that when they are found, they *have* made something of themselves, believably and interestingly.

Tunnel in the Sky is not a bad book, but it is not among Heinlein's best. The second of its flaws is the nature of its hero. By the evidence of this book, if he were to stand in the middle of a desert on a cloudless day, he would attract lightning. He is doubted, struck on the head, flim-flammed, ignored, shoved around, victimized, and treated as an incompetent. He is naive (when asked whether or not he is sexually interested in a girl he goes off on long hunting trips with, he can't even understand the question), and he never, never sees his next lump coming.

At the beginning, his instructor says:

> "I could drop you [from the course]. Perhaps I should."
> "But *why*, sir?"
> "That's the point. I couldn't give a reason. On the record, you're
> as promising a student as I have ever had."

I know the reason. The instructor has nagging doubts about that "Kick Me" sign that Walker wears on his back.

11. 1956

In 1956, Heinlein had his most active year since before the war, publishing three novels. Two were adult novels, his first in five years, and only his second and third since 1942.

Not too long ago, I had reason to look back over all the issues of *Astounding* and *Galaxy* published between 1950 and 1960 in search of stories dealing with politics. The bulk of them were either about dictatorships or about Galactic Empires. The dictatorships were all bad and deserved to be overthrown. If the stories were long enough, they usually were. The Galactic Empires either had Galactic Emperors who stood alone while ministers plotted in the antechambers, or were the home bases for secret corps of political sophisticates that spent their time manipulating native populations for their own good. This is exciting as hell, of course, but it's crude entertainment. Robert Heinlein is one of the very few science fiction writers who have had any experience in practical politics, and this may partly explain his surer and less melodramatic handling of the subject.

Although the central idea of *Double Star* (*Astounding*, February, March and April 1956) is melodramatic—an actor permanently taking the place of a stricken political leader—its development is not melodramatic, but sure and real, because its concern is with the changes that take place within the actor. The story is not a public one, but a private and personal one, and melodrama is not melodrama without a stage to strut on. Put the most flamboyant swashbuckler ever conceived in a prison cell by himself and leave him there, and he has to become something more or the story dies.

What Heinlein envisions is a parliamentary system and empire like that of 19th Century Britain. John Joseph Bonforte is head of a coalition of minor parties whose interests are libertarian: "free trade, free travel, common citizenship, common currency, and a minimum of Imperial laws and restrictions." The main bone of contention is that common citizenship. Bonforte's Expansionists want to include the native populations of Mars and Venus as full citizens within the Empire, while the party in power, the Humanists, take a strict humans-first attitude. Bonforte is about to be made a member of a Martian "nest" when the story begins, and no excuse short of death will be sufficient for him to miss his appointment. Only days before he is due to be adopted a radical splinter group of the Humanist Party kidnaps him, knowing his absence will create exactly the sort of blood-in-the-streets incident that will serve their interests. It is in this situation that an out-of-work actor named Lawrence Smith —"The Great Lorenzo"—is persuaded and pressured to double for Bonforte during the adoption ceremony.

He does this successfully enough, but then Bonforte is turned loose by his captors in such condition that Smith must continue his impersonation. The problem is compounded by the resignation of the Humanist government, meaning that Bonforte's party must form a caretaker government until a general election can be called. Since Bonforte as a person is the only thing that holds the Expansionist coalition together, he *must* be present in person.

Smith, the actor, is originally completely apolitical, Martiandespising, and even cold to the idea of the impersonation he has been inveigled into pulling off. He is also a thorough-going self-admirer. However, once inside the skin of Bonforte, he begins to grow. He learns to respect first the people around Bonforte, and then Bonforte himself. At the end, he is a larger, more pleasant, saner man. Perhaps the lesson is that accomplishment is a matter of both aptitude and the opportunity to demonstrate it.

The story ends when, just as the Expansionists are winning their election, Bonforte dies of a stroke. Smith agrees to carry on in this final role. There is a short afterword written twenty-five years later that indicates Smith's success in becoming Bonforte.

There are a few minor carelessnesses that mar the story a little that might have been eliminated by closer proofreading. For instance, there is a character mentioned on page 20, Doc Scortia, who is never heard of again but who seems to have been replaced by a Doc Capek. There is a story behind that: Heinlein has a physicist friend named Tom Scortia and he wanted to do him the favor of slipping him into a story behind a beard and putty nose. Heinlein then learned that Scortia himself had started writing and selling science fiction, so the manuscript was combed over and the name replaced—in all but one place.

On a different level, I wish that Heinlein had written in greater detail. He has done a fine job of showing the metamorphosis of Smith into Bonforte, and he has described his political system interestingly enough. However, I wish that he had brought the two together more intimately and had let us see more of the political system in action. Smith tells us of it, but we never see more than glimpses of it in closeup. When one of his aides says to him at the end in trying to persuade him to stay on, "Chief, you remember those confounded executive committee meetings? You kept them in line," we can't remember it, because we haven't seen it.

This is a good novel—it won the Hugo award as the best science fiction novel of its year—but if Heinlein had gone into the detail he might have, but did not, this would have been a deeper and far more important novel. As things are, *Double Star* is good light entertainment, but no more than that.

Time for the Stars was the last of Heinlein's Scribner's novels to be illustrated by Clifford Geary. Anthony Boucher thought the story was the best novel of its year and said that the only thing that kept it from being serialized in *F&SF* was that it didn't divide well into parts.

In *The Rolling Stones*, Heinlein's central characters were the twins, Castor and Pollux Stone. Seen from the outside, they present so united a front that it is really not possible to tell one from the other. The hero of *Time for the Stars* is also one of a set of twins, but in this case we see twinhood from the inside and get an entirely different picture of it.

Earth has a population of five billion people when the story opens and a group of twelve starships is about to be sent out to find favorable real estate. Research has turned up the fact that some identical twins can communicate telepathically and that telepathy is not limited to the speed of light, thereby making it a perfect communication medium between Earth and ships that may be gone for as long as a century. The "prison yard whisper" that Tom Bartlett, the hero, and his twin, Pat, have been using for years turns out to be more than they thought it was, and they are signed up by the foundation sponsoring the trip. As a general rule, I have no affection for stories that involve extra-sensory perception. When the stories aren't foolish, which many of them are, the psionics is likely to be so important to the story that normal human motivations and concerns wind up missing entirely. In *Time for the Stars*, however, Heinlein has managed to present telepathy as a major plot element without letting it overwhelm the story.

Partly this is because of the well-developed relationship between Tom and Pat. Pat has more grab and winds up with the shipboard place while Tom is to stay behind on Earth, cut out of the trip. Then Pat has an accident that paralyzes his legs and Tom is back in the picture again. The kicker is that subconsciously neither of them really wants to go on this trip—the ship is fairly certain never to get back safely—and that Pat has won again. Tom's growing understanding of the real nature of his relationship with his twin is the core of the story.

It might not have been, except that again Heinlein has skimped on the finale of his story. It is a catalog of places visited—"'Whistle-Stop' wasn't worth a stop. We're on our way to Beta Ceti, sixty-three light-years from Earth."—of people who die, and of telepathic linkages lost. The story ends with the ship being picked up by a newly-invented faster-than-light ship. Tom meets his latest telepathic linkage, his brother's great-granddaughter, Vicky, who decides to marry him, and the two then prepare to go out to the stars once more. It is, I think, the rushed nature of the last part of the story that made it impossible to serialize.

There are some very lovely things in the story. One is the nature of the organization that sponsors the whole business: the Long Range Foundation.

> The charter goes on with a lot of lawyers' fog but the way the directors have interpreted it has been to spend money only on things that no government and no other corporation would touch ... To make the LRF directors light up with enthusiasm you had to suggest something that cost a billion or more and probably wouldn't show results for ten generations, if ever ...

There is also the idea of limiting family size by imposing quotas and taxing any children over the quota. I understand that this idea has had serious discussion.

Finally, Heinlein tickles my fancy with his account of serendipity, which he defines as digging for worms and striking gold. He then, without pointing it out, demonstrates it beautifully with his faster-than-light ships which are given as the offspring of research done to explain the instantaneous nature of telepathic communication.

Heinlein's third novel in 1956, *The Door Into Summer* (*F&SF*, October, November, December), was another adult story. Like the first two novels, it was written in the first person, though for less obvious reason. A story like *Double Star* of a man changing from one thing to another can probably be told most easily in the first person. Again, the first person certainly makes the difficult difference between identical twins easier to exposit. In a story like *The Door Into Summer*, choice of viewpoint seems to be less central and might have been as easily decided the other way.

There is a certain amount of continuity of thinking in these three books. In all three, for instance, comment is made to the effect that any man has the right to decide when and how he will die. John Joseph Bonforte's ship in *Double Star* is named after Thomas Paine, and so is the hero of *Time for the Stars*. And servo-mechanisms of the sort that are the central interest of *The Door Into Summer* are mentioned in passing in *Time for the Stars*, as though Heinlein had the idea in the back of his mind while writing the earlier book.

Daniel Boone Davis, hero of *The Door Into Summer,* is an engineer in 1970, in partnership with a lawyer friend whom he met in the army. Davis has invented *Hired Girl*, a machine that will clean floors all day long without supervision, and *Window Willie*, a machine to wash windows. He is making a good deal of money, is having the time of his life, is engaged to the company's beautiful and talented secretary, and is about to finish *Flexible Frank*, a machine that will be capable of doing just about any household dirty job. But Davis and his partner are divided—the partner wants to rush *Frank* into production while Davis wants to hold it back until every part is plug-in replaceable. He has no taste for machines that are full of bugs. Davis won't budge, so the partner, whose own taste is for being a wheeler-dealer, and the secretary-fiancée conspire to ease him out of control and out of the company.

You can, by the way, tell that lovely Belle Darkin, the fiancée, is really nasty—she and Davis's cat just don't see eye-to-eye. On the other hand, the partner's eleven-year-old stepdaughter Ricky, Davis, and Davis's cat make a very neat threesome. Little Ricky can't stand Belle, either, showing that her childish instincts are good.

While on a drunken binge following his betrayal, Davis decides to take cold sleep, a suspended-animation process, for thirty years along with his cat so that he can come back and sneer at lovely Belle Darkin when she isn't quite so lovely any more. He signs the papers, but then sobers up and changes his mind. However, when he goes to confront his ex-partner, he stumbles on a piece of information that will blow the whole mess to pieces, so Belle gives him a shot of a hypnotic drug that puts him out of commission, then brings him forward at the proper time for his cold sleep appointment and sends him off on a thirty-year trip to tomorrow.

The story *really* gets complicated from here on. Davis becomes adjusted to the year 2000 and finds he likes it, turns himself into a good engineer again, then stumbles onto a number of bits of evidence that he has done more things back in 1970 than he thought he had. A fellow with a proper time machine is introduced (there is an uncertainty factor—half the time it throws you forward, and half the time it sends you back; but then Davis has reason to think that he *will* go back because he *has* gone back, he has done things in 1970 that he never did the first time around), Davis goads the machine's misanthropic inventor into sending him back to 1970, and once back there, straightens things out. He invents two more machines: a drafting machine and an advanced version of the flexible machine he never finished; he sets things up so that all of his property will go to little Ricky and agrees with her that after she has spent ten years growing up, she will take cold sleep herself and join him in 2001; then he destroys the working model of old *Flexible Frank* to keep it out of the hands of Belle and his ex-partner, collects his cat which was left behind on the night he was shanghaied, and is off again via cold sleep for the year 2001 where he and Ricky and the cat are all joined together in Holy Matrimony.

Time travel stories are generally so complicated that they have to be tightly plotted if they are to be successful, and Heinlein's time travel stories as a group are probably his best constructed. This one is no exception. As a whole, the story is thoroughly melodramatic but very good fun. I imagine that it was a very enjoyable story for Heinlein to write, particularly the nicely-developed engineering ideas. It was as though Heinlein the engineer said, "If I had the parts available, what little gadgets would I most enjoy building?" and then went ahead and built them fictionally. A good story.

12. 1957

That science fiction is particularly difficult to write well has been recognized by almost every critic of the field. Note that I said "to write well." Bad science fiction is very easy to write, which might be why there is so much more of it around. Heinlein himself has gone so far as to say that speculative fiction is the most difficult of all prose forms, and to explain why. John W. Campbell, in his introduction to Heinlein's collection, *The Man Who Sold the Moon*, has also explained why, succinctly and accurately:

> Briefly stated, the science-fiction author must put over to the reader (1), the mores and patterns of the cultural background, (2), interwoven with that—stemming from it, and in turn forcing it into existence—the technological background and then, finally, the characters. He may not use long descriptive passages for any of this necessary material.

These requirements mean that most good science fiction short stories are going to depend on trick endings and gimmicks for their effect. It is difficult enough, God knows, to do the things Campbell is talking about in a novel. In a short story they are almost impossible to do—that is why so many sf shorts depend on stock backgrounds, Galactic Empires and such—and suffer because of it.

I raise the point not for its own interest, but because it throws an interesting light on Heinlein's short story, "The Menace from Earth" (*F&SF*, August 1957). Having given up the short story for the most part, presumably to take advantage of the added room in a novel, Heinlein here returned to it and did a truly brilliant job of presenting a strange background with strange mores—combined with a stock slick fiction plot. Quite the opposite of what you might expect.

The menace of the title is a beautiful third-rate actress in her middle thirties who comes as a tourist to the Moon and temporarily dazzles the boyfriend of Holly Jones, the bright but completely humorless fifteen-year-old narrator of the story. Forget the plot. Luna City is *real*, that's what is important. The jewel of the piece, however, is the account of flying in the city air storage tank, an underground volcanic bubble two miles across. Flying is made possible by air at normal pressure combined with one-sixth normal gravitation. All the trappings are here: wing design (including brand name snobbery for sauce), how the flying works, beginners' areas, rules of the road. The idea is brilliant and believable.

"The Elephant Circuit" (*Saturn*, October 1957) is a mistake, a sloppy, sentimental fantasy that I suspect was written at the very beginning of Heinlein's career and then went without a buyer until 1957. It is about a fat, fatuous, fair-loving retired salesman who spends his time in traveling, attending his beloved fairs. As an excuse to travel, he purports to sell elephants. He is killed in a bus wreck and goes to Heaven to find it a super-fair. His dear dead wife Martha is there, and so is his dear dead dog Bindlestiff, who "had been called away, shortly after Martha." And the salesman is hailed by one and all — at the close he is leading the parade in an elephant-drawn carriage with wife and dog beside him. In the language of the story, you might say that he has Passed On to his Great Reward.

Citizen of the Galaxy (*Astounding*, September, October, November and December) is another of Heinlein's adult juveniles. It is the longest and the last Heinlein story to appear in *Astounding*.

The story is about many things, among them these: slavery seen from the inside, the slave trade, begging, education, spying, anthropology, trading, life in the military, and corporate business. The scale of the story is broad, too: there is the Terran Hegemony, a loose federation three thousand light-years in circumference; and outside this many human and non-human worlds at every level of civilization.

There are properly four parts to *Citizen of the Galaxy*. In the first, Thorby, a small, scared, dirty and sore-covered little boy, is sold as a slave to a one-eyed, one-legged beggar in the city of Jubbulpore, capital of the Nine Worlds, a notorious and repressive little empire outside the Hegemony. Baslim, the beggar, is unusual. During the day he sits at his usual place in the Plaza of Liberty and begs for alms. In his warren at night, he puts on an expensive artificial leg. Over the years he gives the boy a thorough education. He is engaged in some sort of illegal activity, and he sets Thorby to running messages for him, though to what purpose Thorby is not sure. Then Baslim is caught by the Sargon's police and "shortened," and Thorby has to run for cover. He has a set of messages memorized in languages he doesn't understand for delivery to any one of a number of trading ship captains—one of these is in port at the moment and Thorby delivers his message.

The second part of the story takes place aboard the Free Trader "Sisu," and is the longest part of the book. Baslim's message asks, for the sake of the debt owed to him, that the captain take Thorby aboard the ship and treat him as his own until the boy can be delivered to a ship of the Hegemonic Guard, since Baslim has reason to believe that the boy originally came from a planet of the Hegemony. The traders have a very rigid, heavily-stratified society with no place in it for an outsider, so Thorby is accepted with reluctance, and adopted.

Almost as soon as he has succeeded in making a place for himself in the Trader society, however, opportunity and necessity conspire and Thorby is handed on to a ship of the Hegemonic Guard. They have no place for him, either, short of adoption, so he is duly enlisted. At this point, Thorby learns that Baslim was a high officer in the Hegemonic Guard who had gone into the Nine Worlds to report on the slave trade, which the Guard views as pernicious and intolerable. Baslim was allowed to go in only because he could get messages out by way of the Free Traders who owed him a debt for saving some of their people in the same action that had cost him his leg and eye. The begging was his own idea.

As soon as he arrives, the Guard attempts to find out who Thorby is, and eventually succeeds. He turns out to be heir to both a vast fortune and a manufacturing empire on Earth, and accordingly, off Thorby goes again. It takes him some time to discover himself for the fourth time, but finally he succeeds and then is left with a very difficult job to keep him busy.

If this sounds disunited, in some ways it is. Two threads tie it together. The lesser is the process of Thorby's finding a solid and final place where he *fits*—it seems to be his fate to be always a stranger in a strange land, always out of place, always naive. At the end he does have some understanding of himself and what he is doing, and that is a resolution. The second theme is even more solid, as well as typical of Heinlein: freedom and slavery. One of Baslim's conclusions before he lost his head was that one of the largest manufacturers in the Terran Hegemony was abetting the slave trade in the worlds outside. Thorby becomes more and more certain as he learns about Rudbek, the great holding company he has inherited, that this manufacturer is Rudbek itself, and this is one of the reasons he is willing to involve himself in a struggle for corporate power when his inclinations are to chuck the whole thing and go back to the Guard. The company is such a vast amalgam of enterprises that only a few employees in appropriate positions have to be aware of the business the company is involved in. And there is strong reason to believe that Thorby and his parents were originally disposed of because his father, on an inspection trip, was beginning to come too close to the truth. At the end, Thorby is assisting the Guard in developing weapons to make it uneconomical for raiders to attack vessels for slaves and loot, and planning to comb out the lice from Rudbek.

The traders are, if anything, an ironical comment on the problem of freedom. They, the most free in movement, are the least free personally of almost any people, since, in order to live as they do, their society must be very restrictive.

I have some minor bones to pick with the story. It seems an incredible coincidence that Thorby—the lost heir to Rudbek—should ever encounter Baslim. And why does Baslim buy Thorby at all? This happens so early in the story that the reader cannot really assess it, but looking back the question remains unanswered. And finally, the book is clearly disunified—the wrenches from one place to another are almost as severe for the reader as they are for Thorby. However, the book is so successful on so many other counts that these points remain minor.

Citizen of the Galaxy, if not the most successful of Heinlein's juveniles, is certainly the most ambitious. The point of view is an omniscient one—the interest is not just in Thorby or in what Thorby sees, but in Thorby in a context, and the reader sees far more than Thorby does, or any of the characters for that matter. This lifts the book far out of the simple adventure category.

Out of all that is rich and good about *Citizen of the Galaxy*, I want to pick out just two things to mention briefly. One is the elaborate social system of the Free Traders with its moieties, its involved family relationships, its inbred self-satisfaction, its rigidity, and its adoptions of superior talent into the line of command. The other is Heinlein's restraint with Baslim. When you see the character directly, you don't know enough about him and his activities to appreciate him. Appreciation only comes later, and then the character is seen as a man who has been doing a dirty, nasty, difficult job. Heinlein doesn't try to make him glamorous or dashing, and that is admirable restraint.

13. 1958

Heinlein published only two stories in 1958, both juveniles. "Tenderfoot in Space" was a serial in *Boys' Life*; like "Nothing Ever Happens on the Moon" in 1949, it was written directly for the magazine and has never been reprinted in book form. The other story was *Have Space Suit—Will Travel*, which for all its title is a fine book and in my opinion ranks with *Beyond This Horizon* as Heinlein's best work. It is probably the most beautifully constructed story he's ever done.

Although "Tenderfoot in Space" ran for three months in *Boys' Life*, it is no longer than an ordinary novelette of the sort that run two or three to an issue in adult science fiction magazines. The story is about a young Boy Scout and his dog on Venus. The dog is the hero and about a fifth of the story is told from its point of view.

From time to time, almost everybody who reads science fiction finds himself asked by someone who doesn't to recommend a story so that they "can find out what this science fiction stuff is all about." On one hand, you may proudly hand over a story that is completely incomprehensible to anyone who doesn't speak the language, and on the other hand, you can be too careful and hand over something that looks enough like the stories he is used to reading— "It's Great to Be Back," for instance—that the new reader can't see any difference.

My idea of what makes science fiction worth reading is that it prepares people to accept change, to think in terms of change being both natural and inevitable, and that it allows us to look at familiar things from new angles. My choice of a science fiction story to hand a non-reader would be one that combines the unique virtues of science fiction with a comprehensible, attractive, entertaining plot. I give them Robert Heinlein's last novel for Scribner's: *Have Space Suit—Will Travel*.

The novel starts gently enough for anyone unfamiliar with science fiction: there is an eighteen-year-old boy who wants to go to the Moon, and who aims to get there by entering a soap slogan contest with a trip to the Moon as first prize. What he wins is a stripped-down space suit. That isn't quite what he wanted, but he spends a summer putting it into working order in his spare time. Heinlein tells you how he does it and in the process you learn what space suits are like—the account makes the description of space suits in *Rocket Ship Galileo* or any other story you ever read seem elementary—and it is all interesting, all pertinent.

Heinlein's greatest weakness has probably been his story construction. His very earliest stories were badly engineered—an odd criticism to make of an engineer—and even in *Citizen of the Galaxy* you have an example of a story whose parts don't hang together closely. On the other hand, *Have Space Suit—Will Travel* is put together amazingly well. It is pure magic.

Once you have accepted the space suit, the story opens a little: you are taken to the Moon. Once you have accepted the Moon—and Heinlein makes it painfully real; the Moon is his old stomping ground—the story opens again. And then again. First the Moon, then Pluto, then a planet of the star Vega, then the Lesser Magellanic Cloud. Each new place arises out of the last, each new thing implicit in what has gone before. Then the story closes together and comes full circle, back home again.

The difference between this and *Citizen of the Galaxy* is that Thorby becomes a part of each new culture so that it is a wrench to leave it before all the possibilities are explored; the roots of *Have Space Suit—Will Travel* remain on Earth. The traveling simply demonstrates that the world is bigger than it once seemed to be. If you want, you can take it as a guide to acceptance of the whole universe.

It is fun to read. The three main characters are all fine: Kip Russell, the boy with the space suit; Peewee, an exasperating eleven-year-old girl who is smarter than anybody; and the Mother Thing, an alien who is small, furry, warm and protective, like the ultimate Security Blanket, but who is a lot more than that.

For frosting, the story turns a number of science fictional clichés this way and that, as though to show there is a lot of delightful mileage left in them: flying saucers, bug-eyed monsters, the Galactic Council where Earthmen Are Judged—and it has a fine old time in the process. I like to look at the story as the ultimate in fairy tales: the knight errant rides forth to save the fair maiden from the all-time champion dragon—and so what if the damsel is only eleven?

The story is an entertainment, but not a mere entertainment. It has something to say about the value of brains, perseverance, and courage. They aren't lectured about—they are demonstrated and present by implication. They are there if you look. The story is multi-leveled enough to be enjoyed by almost anyone, and it bears re-reading.

Only a misanthrope could dislike *Have Space Suit—Will Travel*. It marks a good end to Heinlein's most productive period.

Bibliography—Heinlein's Second Period

1947

The Green Hills of Earth	*Saturday Evening Post*, Feb. 8, 1947
Space Jockey	*Saturday Evening Post*, April 26, 1947
Columbus Was a Dope	*Startling Stories*, May 1947 (by Lyle Monroe)
It's Great to Be Back	*Saturday Evening Post*, July 26, 1947
Jerry Is a Man (Jerry Was a Man)	*Thrilling Wonder Stories*, Oct. 1947
Water Is for Washing	*Argosy*, Nov. 1947
ROCKET SHIP GALILEO	Scribner's (original juvenile novel)

1948

The Black Pits of Luna	*Saturday Evening Post*, Jan. 10, 1948
Gentlemen, Be Seated!	*Argosy*, May 1948
Ordeal in Space	*Town and Country*, May 1948
BEYOND THIS HORIZON	Fantasy Press (novel, serialized 1942)
SPACE CADET	Scribner's (original juvenile novel)

1949

Our Fair City	*Weird Tales*, Jan. 1949
Nothing Ever Happens on the Moon	*Boys' Life*, April, May 1949
Gulf	*Astounding Science Fiction*, Nov., Dec. 1949
Delilah and the Space-Rigger	*Blue Book*, Dec. 1949
The Long Watch	*American Legion Magazine*, Dec. 1949
RED PLANET	Scribner's (original juvenile novel)
SIXTH COLUMN	Gnome Press (novel, serialized 1941)

1950

Satellite Scout (Farmer in the Sky)	*Boys' Life*, Aug., Sept., Oct., Nov. 1950
Destination Moon	*Short Stories Magazine*, Sept. 1950
The Man Who Sold the Moon	(original story in book of the same title)
FARMER IN THE SKY	Scribner's (juvenile novel, serialized 1950)
THE MAN WHO SOLD THE MOON	Shasta (collection: Life-Line, 1939, "Let There Be Light," 1940; The Roads Must Roll, 1940; Blowups Happen, 1940; The Man Who Sold the Moon, 1950; Requiem, 1940)
WALDO AND MAGIC, INC.	Doubleday (two stories, 1940 and 1942)

1951

Planets in Combat (Between Planets)	*Blue Book*, Sept., Oct. 1951
The Puppet Masters	*Galaxy Science Fiction*, Sept., Oct., Nov. 1951
BETWEEN PLANETS	Scribner's (juvenile novel, serialized 1951)
THE GREEN HILLS OF EARTH	Shasta (collection: Delilah and the Space-Rigger, 1949; Space Jockey, 1947; The Long Watch, 1949; Gentlemen, Be Seated, 1948; The Black Pits of Luna, 1948; "It's Great to Be Back!," 1947; "–We Also Walk Dogs," 1941; Ordeal in Space, 1948; The Green Hills of Earth, 1947; Logic of Empire, 1941)
THE PUPPET MASTERS	Doubleday (novel, serialized 1951)
TOMORROW, THE STARS	Doubleday (anthology, edited by Robert A. Heinlein)
UNIVERSE	Dell (paperback edition of 1941 story)

1952

The Year of the Jackpot	*Galaxy Science Fiction*, March 1952
Tramp Space Ship	*Boys' Life*, Sept., Oct., Nov., Dec. 1952
(The Rolling Stones)	
THE ROLLING STONES	Scribner's (juvenile novel, serialized 1952)

1953

Project Nightmare	*Amazing Stories*, April 1953
Sky Lift	*Imagination*, Nov. 1953
ASSIGNMENT IN ETERNITY	Fantasy Press (collection: Gulf, 1949; Elsewhen, 1941; Lost Legacy, 1941; Jerry Was a Man, 1947)
REVOLT IN 2100	Shasta (collection: "If This Goes On—," 1940; Coventry, 1940; Misfit, 1939)
STARMAN JONES	Scribner's (original juvenile novel)

1954

Star Lummox	*Fantasy and Science Fiction*, May, June, July 1954
(The Star Beast)	
THE STAR BEAST	Scribner's (juvenile novel, serialized 1954)

1955

TUNNEL IN THE SKY	Scribner's (original juvenile novel)

1956

Double Star	*Astounding Science Fiction*, Feb., March, April 1956
The Door Into Summer	*Fantasy and Science Fiction*, Oct., Nov., Dec. 1956
DOUBLE STAR	Doubleday (novel, serialized 1956)
TIME FOR THE STARS	Scribner's (original juvenile novel)

1957

The Menace from Earth	*Fantasy and Science Fiction*, Aug. 1957
Citizen of the Galaxy	*Astounding Science Fiction*, Sept., Oct., Nov., Dec. 1957
The Elephant Circuit	*Saturn*, Oct. 1957
(The Man Who Traveled in Elephants)	
CITIZEN OF THE GALAXY	Scribner's (juvenile novel, serialized 1957)
THE DOOR INTO SUMMER	Doubleday (novel, serialized 1956)

1958

Tenderfoot in Space   *Boys' Life*, May, June, July 1958
Have Space Suit—Will Travel   *Fantasy and Science Fiction*, Aug., Sept.,
                                        Oct. 1958

HAVE SPACE SUIT—
    WILL TRAVEL   Scribner's (juvenile novel, serialized 1958)
METHUSELAH'S CHILDREN   Gnome Press (novel, serialized 1941)

IV. THE PERIOD OF ALIENATION

1. Heinlein's Third Period

From the time that he began to write in 1939, one of the hall-marks of Robert Heinlein's writing has been his concern with facts. He doesn't just like facts, he relishes them, and he sprinkles them through his stories with a liberal hand by means of dialogue, demonstration, and if all else fails, omniscient exposition. There is a very tender line beyond which factual lectures become tedious irrelevancies in fiction, and Heinlein has occasionally come close to this line, but if there is anything that is amazing about his writing it has been his ability to write for, say, ten pages, as he does on space suits in *Have Space Suit — Will Travel*, without losing or even seriously slowing his story.

If there is one thing that marks the six novels published so far in Heinlein's third period, it is a change in those things he has lectured about in his stories. Instead of concerning himself with facts, he has written about the morality of sex, religion, war and politics, but he has treated his opinions as though they were facts. More than this, he has so concentrated on presenting his opinions with every narrative device he knows that he has neglected story construction, characterization, and plot as though they were completely subsidiary to the main business of his opinions-as-facts. Why this change has come, I cannot say exactly, but I suspect a combination of financial independence and a desire to say the things that he most strongly believes has caused Heinlein to pour himself out on paper. The result from an artistic point of view is a mistake.

Certainly, any man's strongly held beliefs will be likely to turn up in his fiction, and most of the ideas that Heinlein has recently presented have previously been present in his fiction, but in reading fiction we can accept these beliefs only if they turn up in certain ways. That is, either a character, acting as spokesman for the author, can present the belief—if it is relevant to the story—or the story itself can serve as a case for the belief. The important point is relevance to the story—a dialogue that continues for five pages, ten pages, or twenty pages, as dialogues have continued in recent Heinlein stories, solely for the purpose of presenting the author's opinions with no necessity for them existing within the story, damned well shouldn't be there.

Let's take an actual example of an idea that Heinlein has put forward on at least five different occasions: Man is a wild animal, the roughest, meanest critter in this neck of the universe. Cross him at your peril.

Heinlein predicts in an ariticle entitled "As I See Tomorrow" in the April 1956 *Amazing* that this point of view will eventually be generally recognized. In its context, this is clearly legitimate. The context is an article giving Heinlein's personal opinions.

The idea appears at the end of *The Puppet Masters*, and again it is clearly legitimate. First, it suits the narrator's character that he should think this: he is a secret agent, used to finding violent solutions to his problems. Second, the opinion comes as a culmination to a set of events that seem to demonstrate its aptness. Third, it is not presented as fact but only as the point of view of the narrator.

In *Starman Jones*, the notion is presented editorially as a comment on the need of beasts of burden to accommodate themselves to man or perish. The idea is tossed off in passing. It is not necessary to the story, but neither is it dwelt upon.

Heinlein's next fictional use of the idea comes in *Tunnel in the Sky*. In this case, it is presented as the opinion of the instructor of the Advanced Survival course. It is in character for him to hold such an opinion and a good part of Heinlein's book is an attempt to make a case—*in action*—for the opinion. I think the case is not made convincingly—within an hour of the start of a survival test scheduled to last from two to ten days, the hero comes on evidence of a murder and theft whose only reason for existence seems to be to provide evidence of man's untrustworthiness—but the opinion is clearly not out of place.

The last appearance of the idea comes in *Starship Troopers*, the first novel written in Heinlein's third period. Heinlein has his narrator "prove" as a class assignment that war and moral perfection derive from the instinct to survive, thereby putting a stamp of approval on war. Rico, the narrator, concludes:

> Man is what he is, a wild animal with the will to survive, and (so far) the ability, against all competition. Unless one accepts that, anything one says about morals, war, politics — you name it — is nonsense. Correct morals arise from knowing what Man *is* — not what do-gooders and well-meaning old Aunt Nellies would like him to be.
>
> The universe will let us know—later—whether or not Man has any "right" to expand through it.

Though it may not seem to be, this is really the old argument that might makes right. It is hard to say whether it is in character for Heinlein's narrator to deliver this argument because the narrator is never defined closely enough for us to tell his attitudes and capabilities. The story itself only partly offers evidence for the argument given: that is, we only know that Heinlein's men are willing to fight. Most important, the argument does not belong of necessity to the story—it is tossed in solely as an off-the-cuff remark. In other words, the presence of this opinion in this story as it is given is of a different order than its presence in either *The Puppet Masters* or *Tunnel in the Sky* and is a digression in a way that it is not in *Starman Jones*. It is frequent extended editorials of this sort that have damaged Heinlein's recent stories beyond any repair.

The impression Heinlein has given by this change in emphasis is of a man standing in a pulpit delivering sermons against an enemy that no one but he can see clearly. Since these opinions he has delivered are obviously of primary importance to him, negative reactions to these stories of his have seemed only to cause him to state his opinions all the more strongly. The novelists of the last century, particularly the bad ones, are difficult and dated reading because they continually moralized and their moralizations have not aged well. My own belief is that Heinlein's moralizations will look just as odd to our descendants and read as poorly.

2. 1959

In 1959, Heinlein published only two stories, a short and a novel, both in *F&SF*, both very interesting. The short, " 'All You Zombies—' " (March 1959), seems to belong in Heinlein's third period for the aggressive way it involves sex and seduction, subjects Heinlein never touched on before but has dealt with more and more frequently in his third period novels.

" 'All You Zombies—' " combines sex and time travel, a very interesting combination indeed, fraught with possibility. Time travel has always fascinated Heinlein, from "Life-Line," his first story, which involved a skinned version of time travel, through *Have Space Suit—Will Travel*, the last story of his second period. The range of switches on the subject that Heinlein has used is vast: men popping into the future, men meeting themselves, men previewing their own deaths. " 'All You Zombies—' " came up with an idea new for Heinlein, but one that had been touched on a few years earlier by Charles Harness.

Harness is a very interesting writer, for all that I doubt that he has published more than a dozen stories all told. His forte has been what James Blish calls the "intensively recomplicated" story (Damon Knight calls it "the kitchen sink technique," which may be more accurate)—the sort of story where idea is piled on idea, complication added to complication, switch thrown on switch, until nobody knows what in hell is happening, not even the author. Most often, because they are so complicated, these stories are done poorly. Van Vogt did them and almost always did them badly, like balance sheets that never added to the same total. Harness was unique in that his stories combined ideas, inventions, insights, complications and extravagances, and still managed to make sense.

One of Harness's best stories was a time travel piece entitled "Child by Chronos."* Its punch was that the main character, a girl, by ducking through a time machine became her own mother. Biologically this doesn't seem to hold water since a child gets only half its genes from each parent and a daughter should be only half what her mother was, not identical. But then, both mother and daughter do have the same parents. It isn't possible to prove Harness wrong. The story is very tricky, and is all the better because the switching around in time is not done solely for the sake of the final effect. There are problems of character involved and the story, with all its switching, solves them quite neatly.

The intensively recomplicated story has never been Heinlein's interest—although "By His Bootstraps" is a neatly composed, if completely empty, example of the type—but " 'All You Zombies—' " combines the intensively recomplicated involutions of a "By His Bootstraps" with an idea that goes Harness one better.

Shorn of its complications, the plot is as follows: In 1945 a one-month-old girl is abandoned on the steps of an orphanage in Cleveland. The girl grows up and at the age of 18 is seduced and left pregnant. It turns out that she is both a functional female and a potentially functioning male. She has the baby, but her female organs are so damaged in the process that they have to be removed and she/he is given hormone shots and turned into a male. The baby, meanwhile, is stolen from the hospital.

The girl-now-boy becomes a confession story writer. After seven years, he is picked up by a bartender with a time machine in his back room and carried back to look for the seducer who done him wrong. The bartender meanwhile hops forward a bit, steals the baby and takes it back to the 1945 orphanage, then hops again to pick up the young man just after he finishes seducing his younger female self. The bartender, who is the young fellow grown older by thirty years, then takes himself forward to 1985 where he recruits his younger self into a time police corps.

* *Fantasy and Science Fiction*, June 1953.

This is a wild story with every knot tied. In about one-quarter of the length of "By His Bootstraps" it comes to a far sharper point and assays out as considerably more of a story.

Biologically, it fires straighter than Harness. Baby, bartender, girl and boy are all one—what other baby could girl and boy have than the one they do?

The end of the story goes even further:

> I *know* where *I* came from—but *where did all you zombies come from?* . . . *You* aren't really there at all. There isn't anybody but me—Jane—here alone in the dark. I miss you dreadfully!

If ever a story was meant to be told in the first person, this is it. In style and denouement it is pure Heinlein; in subject it is a departure.

Starship Troopers (*F&SF*, October, November as *Starship Soldier*), Heinlein's 1959 Hugo award-winning novel, has been widely taken as a militaristic polemic. I don't see that any other reading is really possible. Not only does the story-line actively put the military life in the most glamorous terms possible (note, for instance, the emotional difference between the magazine title, the editor's choice, and the book title, Heinlein's choice), but there are numerous classroom interludes and asides by the narrator that attempt to give a direct philosophical justification for government by veterans, and militarism as a way of life. The book's nearest cousin is the sort of recruiting film that purports to show the life of a typical soldier, with a sound-track commentary by earnest sincere Private Jones who interprets what we see for us. The outstanding characteristic of a film of this sort, and of Heinlein's book, is slick patness.

The story line of this book is actually quite simple: the training of a "Mobile Infantryman" of the future and his participation in a future war. However, Heinlein disguises the simplicity of his story by employing a very involved order of narration that, clarified, goes as follows:

One—Mobile Infantrymen are dropped from a starship during a future war. There is a quick strike, given in detail, ending with the death of one of the armored, heavily-armed soldiers as they are picked up from the raid. This, of course, is just what a recruiting film would do, use a large slab of action as a narrative hook to arouse interest and sympathy, with some death-and-glory to tickle those young adventurers susceptible to its appeal.

Two—Just as the recruiting film would do, cut back to pick up the eager young narrator on the day he enlists (instead of going to Harvard, as his rich father would have him). The next five chapters give an account of basic training: the tough sergeant, the rigorous training, the hero fouling up and being straightened out, and then graduation from basic.

Three—Neatly eased into the above is a flashback to the hero's high school class in History and Moral Philosophy, a course that the society's rulers have decreed must be taken by all (though it need not be passed). There is also a ruling that this course must be taught by an ex-service man, and this class and the hero's teacher, Colonel Dubois, are brought up again and again.

Four—The early career of a raw young soldier. This is where the raid that opens the book naturally fits. Following it is an account of leave and the narrator's application for Officer Candidates School.

Five—A very long chapter showing Rico, the narrator, as an officer-in-training, and then as a student officer in an important combat situation.

Six—Close with the narrator as a seasoned officer in a reprise of the situation that opens the book.

Starship Troopers is in no way an account of human problems or character development. There is no sustained human conflict. The story is the account of the making of a soldier—or, rather, a marine —and nothing more. The narrator goes in as a boot and emerges a lieutenant, and that is all.

Heinlein's "soldiers" *are* really marines, by the way, based on today's Marines, not on regular infantry. They are a small, highly disciplined elite corps with a strong esprit who are carried on board ships run by the Navy, and used on planetary raids. Heinlein's officers are called "mister" and his basic training is called "boot camp," both true of Marines, but not of the Army.

For all that the book is told in the first person, Heinlein's narrator remains curiously anonymous. At the end you know nothing of his tastes, his likes and dislikes, his personal life. The course of the book changes him in no way because there is nothing to change —Rico remains first and last a voice reading lines about how nice it is to be a soldier.

The other characters are even more sketchy, or are simple expositions of an attitude. Rico's father, for instance, is used at the beginning of the book to oppose his son's decision to join the service, and then resurrected as the corporal who replaces Rico when he goes off to OCS (I said the story was pat).

The slickness of the story is quite bothersome to me. War in the story involves death and glory and that is all; disease, dirt, and doubt are missing. All the soldiers we see are tough, smart, competent, cleancut, clean shaven, and noble.

Who is Rico's replacement? His father, of course. Who serves under him as platoon sergeant at the close of the story? His father again, of course. When Rico is fighting as a student officer, who is the sergeant under him? Why, his sergeant from basic training.

When Heinlein introduces a character, it is with this parenthetical paradiddle:

> The Commandant had a permanent rank of fleet general (yes, *that* Nielssen); his rank as colonel was temporary, pending second retirement, to permit him to be Commandant.

Drum flourishes of this sort are frequent and, of course, are irrelevant. Emotion should always be fairly earned, not prompted, forced or manufactured.

It is, of course, Heinlein's intention to make war glorious. He wishes to exalt the military and the common soldier. He says explicitly:

> A soldier accepts personal responsibility for the safety of the body politic of which he is a member, defending it, if need be, with his life. The civilian does not.

In the society of Heinlein's book only ex-servicemen have the right to hold office, to vote, and to teach History and Moral Philosophy, a subject that presumably only they understand. The society is defined as right. Heinlein bulwarks his position by making it the supposed result of "a scientifically verifiable theory of morals," a stacking of the deck that seems an attempt to cut off all debate. I have no final answers myself and I find disturbing the ease with which Heinlein churns out his "right" answers, dismissing all other possibilities.

As an example, Colonel Dubois, who teaches the scientific theory of morals and hence should know what is what, says flatly that value is not an absolute ("Wrong," he says, when Rico guesses it is). Value, according to Colonel Dubois, is only in relation to living persons— value is cost and use; if you value freedom highly you must be willing to give your life for it. A lot of other thinkers, including Plato, have held the opinion that value *is* an absolute, but Dubois is able to dismiss them out of hand. He is *right*, you see, and hence doesn't have to explain, refute, or argue, but simply expound his correct opinions. This, I am all too afraid, is how rigid a government such as Heinlein propounds would actually be. "Our system works better than any used by our ancestors," says another teacher of History and Moral Philosophy, and no doubt his definition of "better," like that of any contented man, is "things as they are," in effect, saying, "Our system is more comfortable and home-like than any used by our ancestors."

In one class in History and Moral Philosophy, the reason is given why this "perfect" government has never been overthrown: "If you separate out the aggressive ones and make them the sheep dogs, the sheep will never give you any trouble." This, to my mind, is the justification of a sheep-shearer. Luckily, of course, Heinlein defines his government as altruistic, and since everything is done by definition in this story, there is nothing to worry about.

I can't help but wonder what the story (recruiting film) would be without a war. The war of the story begins after Rico enters basic and no clear reason is ever given for its start. It is simply needed for illustrative material. Starship troopers are not half so glorious sitting on their butts polishing their weapons for the tenth time for lack of anything else to do.

This book was written to be published by Scribner's as a juvenile, but they refused to accept it, thereby ending their long and profitable association with Heinlein.

3. 1960-1961

In 1960, for the first time since World War II, Robert Heinlein published no fiction. In 1961, he published *Stranger in a Strange Land*, by a good margin his longest book, and a heavily sexual, metaphysical, thoroughly annoying piece of work. It, like *Starship Troopers*, won the Hugo award as the best science fiction novel of its year.

Several years ago, I was asked to write about *Stranger in a Strange Land* but declined because I disliked the book too much to take the page-by-page notes necessary to discuss a story of its complexity. At the time I wasn't any too sure how much of my dislike was because the book was every bit as annoying to me as it was meant to be, and how much was because the book was badly flawed. The first of these is a reaction a critic can't afford.

The book is flawed. It seems to me that Heinlein tells not one, but three stories in this book, and that they do not fit together. There is an adventure story, there is the founding of a new religion, and there is a satire. Potentially the strongest of these is the satire. According to the jacket copy, Heinlein's purpose in writing *Stranger in a Strange Land* "was to examine every major axiom of Western culture, to question each axiom, throw doubt on it—and, if possible—to make the antithesis of each axiom appear a possible and perhaps desirable thing—rather than unthinkable." If that was Heinlein's purpose, I don't think he succeeded. His satire becomes drowned in the other two stories.

In a future year (unspecified, but 1980 as a guess from internal evidence) an expedition of four married couples is sent to Mars and never heard of again. Twenty-five years later a second expedition finds a lone survivor, Valentine Michael Smith, illegitimate offspring of the ship's pilot and Mary Jane Lyle Smith, atomics engineer and inventor of the "Lyle Drive," which powers all modern ships. The young man has been raised by Martians and thinks of himself as one. The Martians think of him as something of an idiot, though by human standards he is quite bright.

Young Smith is heir to his mother's fortune (considerable), his mother's husband's fortune (considerable), his true father's fortune (considerable), and the considerable fortunes of every other member of the first expedition. He also has a pretty good claim under human law of being the sole owner of Mars. As soon as he is brought back to Earth, he is salted away in a hospital and kept incommunicado. An actor is brought in to impersonate him in a television interview.

Ben Caxton, an administration-baiting columnist, begins to think it possible that Smith may be considered dispensable and either killed or kept out of the way in a hospital for the rest of his life, so he and a nurse friend, Jill Boardman, contrive to break Smith out and spirit him away to the protection of a man who is too prominent to be steam-rollered. This man is Jubal Harshaw—doctor, lawyer, and writer of popular trash.

Harshaw takes them in because he feels in the mood for a good scrap, and then in his own elderly, cantankerous, individualistic way settles things so that a very prominent, powerful person—the Secretary General of the Federation, no less—has to worry about the disposition of Smith's financial affairs. This removes Smith from his position as pawn in a power struggle and leaves him free to enjoy himself.

Through the story so far, Mike Smith has been learning more and more of what humans are like and what they do, but his understanding is incomplete. Jubal has three beautiful young secretaries, one of whom, which one we are never sure, initiates Mike into sex. Soon after his independence, he and Jill Boardman leave Jubal's home to travel, Mike working thereafter at a number of jobs. While on this extended trip, he sees monkeys in a zoo picking on one another, and thereupon, according to Heinlein, understands humanity, and incidentally decides to found a new religion.

Ben Caxton goes to visit Mike's temple, becomes shocked at the gang shagging that goes on there (Mike likes sex and has made it an important part of his religion) and leaves hurriedly. Jubal, who explains everything to everybody in the book, explains to Ben: 1) when you go into somebody's home you have to accept the way they do things, and 2) you're just jealous because Jill is sleeping around. Ben goes back and tries again and finds that he likes it this time.

Finally even old Jubal goes to take a look. He likes it all, too.

Mike, by choice, then allows himself to be martyred by an angry crowd. We have, however, good reason to believe that his religion will prevail.

The story does have its moments. At one point there is a very bright television commercial advertising a contraceptive (Wise Girl Malthusian Lozenges). There is the idea of Fair Witnesses, people trained in objective witnessing and hired to do it. There are the Fosterites, a religious group, who use salesmanship, slot machines, temple dancing, sex, and temple saloons, and sell their own products:

> "Always look for that happy, holy seal-of-approval with Bishop Digby's smiling face on it. Don't let a sinner palm off on you something 'just as good.' Our sponsors support us; they deserve your support."

Moreover, they use strong-arm techniques to crush opposition and forcefully assist certain brethren who leave wills in favor of the church to attain Heaven sooner than they might have otherwise.

As an interesting sidelight: At the 1962 World Science Fiction Convention, Theodore Sturgeon told of a time when he had run out of ideas and Heinlein came to his rescue with twenty-six story ideas and a check. Sturgeon used a number of the ideas, giving credit to Heinlein indirectly by including characters sporting one or another of Heinlein's pen names. One of the stories, entitled "And Now the News . . ."* was about a man whose overconcern for the daily news drove him crazy. Heinlein includes that idea here in passing:

> "Remind me," Jubal told her, "to write an article on the compulsive reading of news. The theme will be that most neuroses can be traced to the unhealthy habit of wallowing in the troubles of five billion strangers."

---

* *Fantasy and Science Fiction*, Dec. 1956.

The adventure story lies in the first half of the book: spiriting Mike to safety and winning him his freedom and inheritance. The satire lies in showing how men look to a Martian. The third story is the founding of Mike's religion.

Unfortunately, founding a religion is not all there is. I've left out Mike's Martian-trained ability to do almost anything. James Blish puts it like this:

> He can control his metabolism to the point where any outside ob-server would judge him dead; he can read minds; he is a telekinetic; he can throw objects (or people) permanently away into the fourth dimension by a pure effort of will, so easily that he uses the stunt often simply to undress; he practices astral projection as easily as he undresses, on one occasion leaving his body on the bottom of a swimming pool while he disposes of about thirty-five cops and almost as many heavily armored helicopters; he can heal his own wounds almost instantly; he can mentally analyze inanimate matter, well enough to know instantly that a corpse he has just encountered died by poisoning years ago; levitation, crepitation, intermittent claudication, you name it, he's got it—and besides, he's awfully good in bed.*

Mike's ability to do almost anything and the similar abilities of the followers of his religion make his religion right by definition, as Heinlein's government of veterans in *Starship Troopers* was right by definition, and hence trivial.

If you grant the story's premises, the religion cannot be argued with, just as, if I were to write a story in which Heaven was only open to string savers and mud eaters and actually made things come out that way, my religion would be beyond argument. You can't argue with facts, and Heinlein has made the rightness of his religion a fact.

As nearly as I can tell, however, the story's premises are not true: there are no Martians of the sort Heinlein writes of, and no super powers are available to those who think proper Martian thoughts. And without these anyone who attempts to practice the book's religion (which includes mass sexual relations) is headed for trouble. In other words, the religion has no point for anybody.

Both story and religion, it seems to me, would be much sharper

* *The Issue at Hand*, p. 69.

without the rather silly things that Smith is capable of doing. Smith's education and enlightenment should be central but they aren't—instead, Smith's ability to control the length of his haircut by thinking is central, and that has no importance whatsoever.

Those capable of accepting Mike's religion (an ability inborn in one person in a hundred) and developing super powers are God, the only God there is, so it seems. Since they are God, they continue to be God after death—the book calls death "discorporation." They run the universe they have invented (how, why, and from where, like so much of all this, are unanswered) and for no good reason wear wings and halos. This construction of things seems to render all human action in the story completely irrelevant, but let that go. It also seems pretty foolish as story material, but let that go, too.

Heinlein's concern with his religion is so great, unfortunately, that he lets all character development go hang. Mike Smith is lessened by his super powers. (And considering that Heinlein demonstrates his awareness of the meaning of names in this book, it is no accident that Smith's names are "Valentine"—for its sexual connotation in our culture, not its explicit meaning—and "Michael," meaning "who is like God.") Jubal Harshaw, too, is lessened by his super powers—doctor, lawyer, etc.; his multiple training seems a gratuitous gift from Heinlein without reason or explanation. He redeems himself somewhat by his crusty nature, but I find him suspect. He is too pat.

Some of the minor characters have life at the beginning of the story and then lose it, overcome by the flood of talk that engulfs the last half of the novel. Which secretary sleeps with Mike his first time out? They are so lacking in definition that it is impossible to tell. Jill Boardman supposedly loves Ben Caxton, but won't sleep with him. She will, however, go off around the country with Mike on a sleep-in basis. Why? I can't say. At any time it would not surprise me for her to unscrew her foot and stick it in her ear—she is capable of anything. Ben Caxton's motivations are equally unclear.

Those parts of the satire and the religion that can be applied to human beings in a normal situation—and that is the only kind of satire that has any meaning—are sharp enough to cut. It is almost impossible to read *Stranger in a Strange Land* without bleeding a little, which is, of course, a very good reason for reading it. It may also be the reason that it has sold the least well of any of Heinlein's third period novels.* If this is so, it is too bad, because for all that I am disappointed in the book, for all that it is imbalanced, *Stranger in a Strange Land* is worthy of respect.

4. 1962-1964

In 1962, the Hoffman Electronics Corporation ran a series of six science fiction stories as advertisements in *Scientific American* and other magazines: two by Isaac Asimov and one each by A. E. van Vogt, Fritz Leiber, Frank Riley, and Robert Heinlein. Heinlein's story, "Searchlight" (August, 1962), is about a blind girl lost on the Moon. The story is very brief. The idea is interesting, but the story is overly condensed for the emotional impact it is meant to carry.

Heinlein's next three novels, *Podkayne of Mars*, *Glory Road*, and *Farnham's Freehold*, are not at all successful and, unlike *Stranger in a Strange Land*, command very little in the way of respect. It almost seems that Heinlein, in the attempt to plead special cases, has forgotten most of the things he once knew of story construction and has come full circle to the point he once started from.

Podkayne of Mars is, with *Rocket Ship Galileo*, the least of Heinlein's juveniles. In some ways, it is a return to Heinlein's first novels for Scribner's. Like them, and unlike his more recent books, his lead is only fifteen years old, a dependent child. This immediately limits the scope of the book.

The main character of the story is a young girl. Anthony Boucher in his round-up review of 1963 science fiction books in *The 9th Annual of the Year's Best SF* hailed the story in these terms:

> The first 1963 Heinlein, and one of his best in many years, was
> *Podkayne of Mars*, a shrewd and successful effort to widen the s-f
> audience by a teen-age heroine. Poddy's first-person narrative re-
> veals her as a genuinely charming girl (perhaps the most delightful
> young female in s-f since Isaac Asimov's Arkady Darell), and her

---

* Perhaps no longer true, in view of the hippie vogue for *Stranger*.

creator as the master absolute of detailed indirect exposition of a future civilization.

I couldn't agree less.

I do agree that there is a place for young girls in science fiction (as well as old men, middle-aged women and any other advance over young men aged 20-30), but I don't think Heinlein has filled it. I find Poddy no more charming than I found Arkady Darell, the central character in *Second Foundation*, Asimov's novel. In fact I can think of only two truly delightful young female characters in modern science fiction and those are Pauline Ashwell's Lizzy Lee from a very good story, "Unwillingly to School,"* and Heinlein's own Peewee Reisfeld from *Have Space Suit—Will Travel*.

Moreover, *Podkayne* is not really a first-person narrative. It is a journal kept by Poddy with occasional marginal notes by her younger brother Clark. I can think of two faults in this. One is that journals kept by fifteen-year-old girls are likely to be filled with gush and irrelevance. This means that any resulting book is likely to be a poor story, or an unconvincing journal. Heinlein has chosen to write a convincing journal. The other fault is that the journal is kept while the action is going on, not written afterward in one piece, and the result is that we are jerked from one actionless moment that provides the peace needed for writing to another, fed corrections of things we have been told before, and in general exposed to a helter-skelter narrative. Fine again as a journal.

Poddy's lack of charm for me is the product of a kind of handling that no previous Heinlein juvenile protagonist has ever had. I suspect simply that Heinlein does not feel comfortable writing in the person of a female character. Poddy is given to setting down sentences like:

> At first I thought that my brother Clark had managed one of his more charlatanous machinations of malevolent legerdemain.

and

> I got kissed by boys who had never even *tried* to, in the past—and I assure you that it is not utterly impossible to kiss me, if the project is approached with confidence and finesse, as I believe that one's instincts should be allowed to develop as well as one's overt cortical behavior.

* *Astounding Science Fiction*, Jan. 1958.

Her expressions of vituperation are "dandruff," "dirty ears," "*spit*," and "snel-frockey." Above all, she is incredibly coy. She refers to one character throughout as "Miss Girdle FitzSnugglie," generally shortened to "Girdie."

Even less appealing, and less likely, is Poddy's eleven-year-old brother, Clark, who, like an earlier Heinlein-described child—little Ricky in *The Door Into Summer* who at six could not bear to be touched—is thoroughly sick. Clark is totally asocial and has an insatiable desire for masses of money, an obvious love substitute. In the earlier case, Heinlein apparently didn't realize the sickness of his character, but here he makes mention of it at the end of the story. It is, in fact, the only claim to a point that the story has.

The unlikelihood of Clark, who is the novel's true central character, is not in his sickness but in his catalog of abilities. His IQ is given by Heinlein as 160, which is fairly high, but not all that rare. However, at the age of eleven he can: (1) tumble, (2) operate a slide rule, (3) read lips expertly, (4) win piles of cash from "unbeatable" gambling houses any time he cares to, (5) do expert photography, (6) unhoax a time bomb, (7) be a successful smuggler, (8) read English (a foreign language) that is written in Martian Oldscript (a script known only to experts), (9) break into secret diaries and leave messages written first in ink visible only under ultraviolet light, and then in ink that becomes visible only after two days, (10) break into a sealed delivery robot, rewire it to do what he wants it to, leave no traces, and completely baffle the manufacturer of the robot in the bargain, (11) separate dyes from film, given as a thing ordinarily possible only to a master chemist working in a special laboratory, and (12) kill a large adult woman with his bare hands.

There is no real story for two-thirds of the book. Poddy and Clark set out from Mars to Earth, stopping on Venus on the way, in company with their Uncle Tom, who is to represent Mars at an important triplanetary conference. Shortly after they all arrive on Venus, Poddy and Clark are kidnapped by some people who wish Uncle Tom to follow their particular line at the conference. Knowing their Uncle Tom will not change his vote under pressure and that they will be killed by their captors, the kids escape. Period.

Glory Road is a sword-and-sorcery fantasy, a second cousin of Jack Vance's excellent *The Dying Earth*, of Robert E. Howard's Conan stories, and of Edgar Rice Burroughs' stories of Mars. In fact, it is dedicated to the readers of *Amra*, an amateur magazine that is devoted to a celebration of sword-and-sorcery fantasy. *Glory Road*, unfortunately, doesn't share the color, atmosphere, action and good fun of its models. Instead it spends the bulk of its energy on conversation about the relativity of customs, the second-rate nature of sex as practiced on this planet (Earthmen are Lousy Lovers), Earth as the *only* place in Twenty Universes where prostitution is practiced, the primitive nature of democracy and its ineffectiveness as a system of government, and similar topics. The sword-and-sorcery fantasy merely comes as an interlude in the conversation, as though clowns were to pummel each other with bladders as an entr'acte on *Meet the Press*.

The narrator of the story is Evelyn Cyril "Oscar" Gordon, ex-college football star, newly-discharged veteran of the fighting in Southeast Asia, hero in the making. He is recruited by an ad in the Paris edition of the *Herald Tribune* for a job as hero—not realizing that Professional Heroes are silly asses at best and at worst causes of more destruction than they ever know. But Gordon shows himself throughout to be an unbright malcontent and the point escapes him. The job he takes promises high pay, glorious adventure and great danger. His recruiters are a handsome young woman (whom Oscar soon marries) and a runty old geezer (who turns out to be the young woman's grandson).

The three of them pop through to an alternate universe where Gordon is handed, in between conversations, a number of cardboard monsters to dispose of. This is his training for a final swordfight that wins "the Egg of the Phoenix," the lost property of the girl. It is then revealed that the girl is top dog of the aforementioned Twenty Universes. Oscar mopes around with nothing to do for sixty pages and then goes back home. At the end, he is prepared to go out looking for more adventure.

A minimum of one-third of this 288-page book, exclusive of conversations, has no reason for existence, since it does not affect the main goal of the story, the winning of the Egg. It establishes merely that Oscar doesn't like our present world, that sitting around after he has won the Egg doesn't suit him, either, and that after coming home again, he is still unhappy.

Beyond that, of course, the interminable conversations do nothing but demonstrate Heinlein's pet notions, again given protection from attack by being called "facts." They have nothing to do with the adventure, and hence don't belong in the book.

Finally, the procession of adventures does not build to a climax. Monsters simply appear every so often to be disposed of by Oscar. Even the fight for the Egg of the Phoenix lacks the bounding appeal it ought to have, because we only learn afterward what it is and why it is worth fighting for. At the time it is won, it is simply a name, a meaningless bibble-bibble.

Enough doubt eventually penetrates Oscar's mind after the adventures are over that he goes to visit the old grandson who was his companion in adversity to ask him if what he went through was really necessary. The old fellow assures him that it was, and this is enough for Oscar. It seems to me that more compelling evidence is demanded, however, and it isn't in the story.

The protagonist of *Farnham's Freehold* is Hugh Farnham, a well-to-do, self-educated contractor and all-around-competent-man. The other central characters are his wife Grace, their son Duke and daughter Karen, Karen's sorority sister Barbara (a divorcee), and their houseboy Joe, a Negro accounting student.

The time of the story is the near future. We are at the height of an international crisis that turns into a nuclear war while the family is sitting around after dinner playing bridge. Mountain Springs, the scene of the story and clear analogue of Colorado Springs, Heinlein's home town at the time of writing, is a prime military target. Consequently the bridge game is adjourned to Farnham's well-equipped sub-basement bomb shelter where Barbara plays out and wins the most incredible fictional bridge hand of all time:

seven no-trump, doubled, redoubled and vulnerable, a side bet riding.

Three bombs are dropped on them, the third while Farnham and Barbara, who have just met, are making love in the back room. The third bomb kicks them into what they believe is an alternate universe (it turns out to be the far future). The location of the house is exactly what it always was, but the climate is now subtropical and the country wild. They make a life for themselves, though Karen dies in childbirth, something Grace, who is an alcoholic, blames her husband for, although it can hardly be called his fault.

At this point, they are discovered by the local rulers, who are Negroes. Whites are slaves and table-meat, and so they are made slaves. Farnham makes a nice place for himself by translating books and turning present-day games into marketable items for his new master. Barbara bears Farnham twins as a result of that one night in the back room, and does what Farnham tells her to do. The rest of the original group have each gone to hell in their own particular way: Joe, the Negro accounting student, has become a part of the local power structure and is perfectly content; Grace is the master's fat little pussycat; and Duke has been castrated and turned into a household pet.

Farnham eventually decides to run for the hills with Barbara and the twins, but they are caught before they get out of the palace. Their master decides to be generous with them and send them back where they came from in a genuine time machine that his scientists have whipped up.

They land back in Mountain Springs the night that the bombs fell and scoot out of town, headed for an abandoned mine that Farnham owns. When the bombs stop falling, they set up a store in a little enclave bounded from the world by mine fields and protected by rifles. And since this world varies slightly from their original world, they have the hope that the future need not be finally determined to be the one they have just come from.

The minor characters—everybody but Farnham—are just defined enough to seem odd. Karen cheers when her father and her friend come out of the back room, and then dies in childbirth. Barbara mindlessly does what Farnham tells her to do. Grace is a fat, fatuous, useless lush. Duke is tied to his mother by a silver umbilical cord, takes up a narcotic drink at first opportunity, and doesn't mind being castrated because it puts him in a more secure position.

Farnham himself is one great big inconsistency. He is a libertarian who orders people around at gunpoint. He threatens quite seriously to kill his son when Duke won't obey him, and then becomes hysterical when Duke willingly lets himself be castrated. Most important, for all that he is the archetype of the competent man, he has done not one thing to avert the global war he has seen coming. In fact, he is a very odd candidate for the title of competent man: he botches everything from his familial relations to the escape attempt.

These familial relations are very odd, too. Barbara first becomes attracted to him for the way he handles his family, but look at the family: a lush, a momma's boy and a daughter home pregnant from college. (Barbara later assures him that the family is not his fault.) If Heinlein is aware of any inconsistency, he doesn't show it.

It is interesting that for all the concern with liberty and competence that Heinlein demonstrates in this story, his characters do not actually determine anything that happens. They suffer attack, are blown into the future, are found, are sent home again. They remain passive, suffering and impotent throughout. The story is almost a study in the varieties of impotence. The nasty future regime is not caused by the characters, affected by the characters, or disturbed by their leaving. The final situation, in fact, seems like nothing so much as an attempt to keep from being the subject of further manipulation by an implacable universe, an attempt on Farnham's part to be for once the cause of events: "World stay out or be blasted in two! In Farnham's Freehold, Farnham rules."

Only one story purpose emerges in the end that makes any sense: Heinlein's characters survive. Survival at all costs is a theme that is very important to Heinlein, but it fails to carry this book because the survival they achieve is not the triumph Heinlein thinks it is. Heinlein thinks he is talking of liberty when he is really talking only of life; liberty becomes redefined as "living to suit myself"; that is all that Farnham achieves, but it is enough to content him.

5. 1965-1967

Over the years, Heinlein had gathered his short stories and published them in some half-dozen collections. In the middle 1960's only a handful remained unreprinted, including two stories from *Boys' Life* of no great interest to adults and several stories from his earliest years like " 'My Object All Sublime' " that might better be forgotten.

However, Ace Books, a paperback house, noticed that enough material remained unreprinted in paperback to make a readable collection, and contacted Heinlein. The resulting book contained five stories, including one new one, together with an introduction that was a modified version of a Heinlein article originally published in *Galaxy* in 1952. The book appeared in early 1966 under the title *The Worlds of Robert A. Heinlein*.

The new story was a short novelette entitled "Free Men." It apparently had received no welcome from the science fiction magazines, which is understandable since the story is not economically told and is sketchy in detail. The plot is reminiscent of Heinlein's early novel *Sixth Column* in which a few men throw out an Oriental invasion force. The plot in that case was John Campbell's, and it seems possible that Heinlein was impelled by his sense of realism to re-examine the theme. In any case, "Free Men" is about a guerilla band in an occupied post-atomic war America. The band is betrayed and their leader killed, but at the end they determine to carry on, even though they have no visible prospects of winning, because that is the sort of thing that free men do.

One other unpublished story of Heinlein's was proposed for the collection, but was ultimately not included because it was not science fiction.

The Moon Is a Harsh Mistress, Heinlein's most recent novel, was serialized in *If* in late 1965 and early 1966, and won him his fourth Hugo award for best novel. Line-by-line, it is fascinating reading. I suspect that Heinlein could even write laundry lists that would be entertaining to read. Moreover, *The Moon Is a Harsh Mistress* is less flawed by sermons and constructional weakness than the other books of his third period. I must admit, however, that fascinating as I find it, I don't think *The Moon Is a Harsh Mistress* is a good or effective novel. It is, moreover, almost as marked with symbols of resignation, doubt and defeat as *Glory Road* and *Farnham's Freehold*.

The plot line of this, the second longest of Heinlein's novels, is simple enough. Like Heinlein's first novel and so many others since, it is a story of revolution. In 2075, Luna is a penal colony, a dumping ground for transportees, much as Australia was at the beginning of the last century. Because of irreversible physiological changes (so Heinlein says—for once he skimps on justification and I would have been interested to be shown his evidence) these transportees are unable to return to Earth when their sentences have been served. Luna raises grain for an over-populated and undernourished Earth which continues to shove convicts at her, but which returns next to nothing in the way of goods for the food it receives. In short, and in general, Luna is being victimized.

The large computer that co-ordinates almost everything on the Moon estimates seven years before food riots take place on the Moon, followed by cannibalism and social disintegration, and Earth just will not *listen*. It is happy with things as they are and sees no reason why Luna should not be, too. In fact, the people on Earth are almost infuriatingly smug. The only answer is revolution, and the novel follows the Lunar Revolution from the foundation of the nuclear cell in the revolutionary organization to capitulation by the Federated Nations of Earth.

The Moon Is a Harsh Mistress is totally a story of process rather than character. Heinlein has always been more interested in how machines and societies work than in why people act, and this is probably more true of this novel than any of his others. And it is the center of what is wrong with it as a story. There is wonderful material here on the organization and implementation of a revolution. In fact, if I ever had to run a revolution, I think I might well consult this book. It is this expertise and Heinlein's skill at phrase-turning that give this book its line-by-line fascination. However, because this is a book about the workings of things rather than the workings of people, it is ultimately flat and a failure as a story. It is a handbook, not a novel. Heinlein tries with great skill to inject drama into *The Moon Is a Harsh Mistress*, but the devices he uses do not bear examination or are such obvious appeals for unearned emotion that they irritate rather than captivate.

Heinlein has always had a weakness for forcing emotion, possibly because his characters themselves are unemotional. When Heinlein wants us to approve a character or a position, or to feel moved, instead of giving us a natural emotional reason growing out of the story or, alternatively, underplaying, he is all too likely to try to find a button in us to push. One example appears in the scene in the book version of *"If This Goes On—"* where an old man stands to speak in assembly against the use of psychological re-conditioning. First, we are told that he looks like Mark Twain. That's a button. Then, we are told that the end of his speech is punctuated by him dropping dead. That's another button. In truth, if a writer wants an emotional response from his readers, he should be expected to work for it. The bid for emotion has to be placed in a context. If I say, "Beth died," it would be foolish to expect my readers to break out their hankies. If I say, "Beth, a big-eyed little girl with pipestem legs, was wantonly killed by a drunken Nazi butcher. As they dragged her forlorn body away, her schoolbooks lay spilled in the gutter," that is forcing sentiment by obvious appeals. If I want my readers to cry, I've got to provide them with reasons for liking Beth and solid reasons for her death.

However, and most particularly in *The Moon Is a Harsh Mistress*, Heinlein's appeals to emotion don't arise legitimately out of his context. That is completely filled with the mechanics of revolution. Instead he follows the middle course outlined in the last paragraph and from time to time breaks out a bugle or a violin. He plays for a paragraph and then puts his instrument away again.

The title of the novel, for instance, is a ringing phrase that means not very much in particular, and exactly nothing in relation to this book. *The—Moon—Is—a—Harsh—Mistress*. Hear the bugle?

Or this:

> Station was mobbed and I had to push through to see what I assumed to be certain, that passport guards were either dead or fled.

"Dead" it turned out, along with three Loonies. One was a boy not more than thirteen. He had died with his hands on a Dragoon's throat and his head still sporting a little red cap.

This is effective writing. There is no question of that. It is also basically shoddy. I don't believe that in the entire history of the world a boy not more than thirteen has attacked a soldier with his bare hands and "died with his hands on a Dragoon's throat and his head still sporting a little red cap." If Heinlein had said the boy skulled a guard at thirty paces with a rock and got shot as a consequence, I'd believe that, but "Dragoons" and "little red caps" are the devices of propaganda.

The date of the story is deliberately chosen for resonance with the American Revolution. The Lunar Declaration of Independence is settled on the 2nd of July, 2076, and announced on the 4th. In one sense you can say that this was intelligent capitalization on historical sentiment by the Loonies, but in actual fact it is nothing more than Heinlein doing a bit of auctorial cheating. The sentiment being capitalized upon is not that of the North American Directorate in 2076—it is your sentiment now. The closer the similarity between one revolution and the other, the more obvious it is that Heinlein is trying to fife-and-drum us into accepting what we would not otherwise find moving, and when he says, "A dinkum comrade, Foo Moses Morris, co-signed much paper to keep us going—and wound up broke and started over with a little tailoring shop in Kongville," he isn't talking about the Lunar Revolution at all. He's talking about Robert Morris, financier of the American Revolution, who died in poverty, and as a consequence I somehow just can't quite accept "Foo Moses Morris," who never appears again, as being real. Notice, too, that when Heinlein wants to jerk a tear he throws in the word "little." Not just a tailoring shop, but a "little" tailoring shop; not just a red cap, but a "little" red cap.

Heinlein also tries to give his story dramatic force by tying it onto the tail of another of his novels, *The Rolling Stones*. An important character in that book is Hazel Meade Stone, and a moderately prominent (but not important) one in *The Moon Is a Harsh Mistress* is a young girl named Hazel Meade, who eventually marries a young tough named Stone. Apparently your affection and interest in her earned in *The Rolling Stones* is supposed to pay Heinlein's way in this novel. The only trouble is that it is impossible for the Lunar society of *The Rolling Stones* to be derived from the supposedly previous society of *The Moon Is a Harsh Mistress*, and it is impossible for the Hazel Meade Stone of one book to be the Hazel Meade Stone of the other. (See pages 184-185 and 190 of *The Rolling Stones* just to start.) Heinlein doesn't care about this— he is interested only in the effect of the tag "Hazel Meade Stone."

The Lunar society that Heinlein creates doesn't seem completely self-consistent. For one thing, he states that half the newcomers to Luna die with reasonable immediacy: "Luna has only one way to deal with a new chum: Either he makes not one fatal mistake, in personal behavior or in coping with environment that will bite without warning . . . or he winds up as fertilizer in a tunnel farm." Yet he produces Lunar idiots and asses to suit his purposes, exactly the people one would think *would* make fatal mistakes. Moreover, he has a number of very idealistic marital systems that horrify North Americans, but which newcomers accept readily, the systems being based on the Heinlein-given fact of two million men and one million women on the Moon. But women are given as being protected and half of the newcomers die, so Heinlein says. One would think that would tend to balance things. Only five per cent of the population, again according to Heinlein, is actually convict. One would think that, as with the Mormons who immediately attracted many more women than men, in a reasonably short period the natural balance of children would assert itself, and by the time free citizens made up ninety-five per cent of the population, the numbers would be approximately even again. The narrator of the book is a *third-generation* Loonie and the imbalance is still two to one. None of this seems to bear examination.

The most obvious device that Heinlein uses to manufacture suspense is patently artificial. One of the four members of the original cell, and the whole-hearted coordinator of the revolution, is the computer mentioned earlier, named Mike. The notion of a sentient computer is not particularly objectionable in itself, except for the consequent diminishing in stature of the human characters. However, at the beginning of the story the computer announces the odds against success are seven to one. Thereafter, at frequent intervals, new odds are announced, getting longer and longer until they eventually reach a hundred to one. Throughout, however, to our apparent view things are going exactly as planned. We have to take Heinlein's word that things are actually getting worse. One would think, too, that the initial odds would have taken into account all the necessary chances the revolution has to take, and that only the unexpected would materially affect the odds. The unexpected does not seem to happen, but the odds—Heinlein's computer tells us—keep getting longer and longer. The result is an altogether unreal sort of suspense that lacks the power to compel belief.

The most irritating device that Heinlein has used in the book, however, is the language it is told in. The narrator thinks and writes in a sort of babu-Russian in which the first-person pronouns and definite articles are all but missing. This is bothersome to read in itself, but it is also both artificial and irrelevant. First, it is not consistent either with itself or with actual Russian grammatical construction. (Buttonhole a passing Russian and check the book out with him.) Second, by 2075 one assumes that everybody will talk enough differently from the present to need translation into our terms. The future equivalent of "damn," expressed in present terms, is "damn." If one assumes that in 2075 English is spoken on the Moon with a Russian grammatical structure, it will not sound *then* like an ignorant present-day Russian trying to speak English. It will sound "normal," and therefore should be represented by normal English, with perhaps an odd word or two for flavor. Third, and reinforcing this point, it is a fact that the narrator is the only character in the whole book who speaks this artificial jargon. It would have better been dispensed with.

Part of the problem is that this main character is a cipher. The computer is much more alive and forceful. (Note, too, that the computer, like the main character of *Stranger in a Strange Land*, is named Mike, which—as has already been pointed out—means "who is like God," a point Heinlein is well aware of.) The only claims that the protagonist has to individuality are his one arm and his dialect. Other than that, he is faceless, even more so than the similar narrator of *Starship Troopers*, and where Rico of *Starship Troopers* can act decisively, the present hero does not and cannot. Manuel does nothing throughout *The Moon Is a Harsh Mistress* but report the progress of the revolution. He is an observer, but he does not himself act. In fact, at the one point in the story at which he is called upon to act—to initiate the defense of the Moon against a sneak attack in his capacity as Minister of Defense—he is not present and not able, and the computer, which overshadows him throughout, imitates his voice and issues his orders for him. The narrator has no opinions of his own, no tastes, no individual will—he is exactly the person to be replaced by a sentient computer.

The Moon Is a Harsh Mistress has its interest, but it is not as a novel. It is as dramatized lecture.

Bibliography—Heinlein's Third Period

1959

"All You Zombies—"   *Fantasy and Science Fiction*, March 1959
Starship Soldier   *Fantasy and Science Fiction*, Oct., Nov.,
  (Starship Troopers)   1959
THE MENACE FROM EARTH   Gnome Press (collection: The Year of the
                               Jackpot, 1952; By His Bootstraps, 1941;
                               Columbus Was a Dope, 1947; The Men-
                               ace from Earth, 1957; Sky Lift, 1953;
                               Goldfish Bowl, 1942; Project Night-
                               mare, 1953; Water Is for Washing, 1947)
STARSHIP TROOPERS   Putnam (juvenile novel, serialized 1959)
THE UNPLEASANT PROFESSION
  OF JONATHAN HOAG   Gnome Press (collection: The Unpleasant
                               Profession of Jonathan Hoag, 1942;
                               The Man Who Traveled in Elephants,
                               1957; "All You Zombies—," 1959;
                               They, 1941; Our Fair City, 1948; "And
                               He Built a Crooked House," 1940)

1960

no fiction published

1961

STRANGER IN A STRANGE LAND	Putnam (original novel)

1962

Searchlight	*Scientific American*, Aug. 1962, and other magazines (advertisement)
Podkayne of Mars	*If*, Nov. 1962, Jan., March 1963

1963

Glory Road	*Fantasy and Science Fiction*, July, Aug., Sept. 1963
GLORY ROAD	Putnam (novel, serialized 1963)
PODKAYNE OF MARS	Putnam (juvenile novel, serialized 1962-3)

1964

Farnham's Freehold	*If*, July, Sept., Oct. 1964
FARNHAM'S FREEHOLD	Putnam (novel, serialized 1964)
ORPHANS OF THE SKY	Putnam (collection: Universe, 1941; Common Sense, 1941)

1965

The Moon Is a Harsh Mistress	*If*, Dec. 1965, Jan., Feb., Mar., Apr. 1966
THREE BY HEINLEIN	Doubleday (omnibus: The Puppet Masters, 1951; Waldo, 1942; Magic, Inc., 1940)

1966

Free Men	(original short story in THE WORLDS OF ROBERT A. HEINLEIN)
THE MOON IS A HARSH MISTRESS	Putnam (novel, serialized 1965-6)
THE WORLDS OF ROBERT A. HEINLEIN	Ace Books (paperback collection: Free Men, 1966; Blowups Happen, 1940; Searchlight, 1962; Life-Line, 1939; Solution Unsatisfactory, 1940)

1967

THE PAST THROUGH
   TOMORROW

Putnam (the Future History, revised and
nearly complete: Life-Line, 1939; The
Roads Must Roll, 1940; Blowups Hap-
pen, 1940; The Man Who Sold the
Moon, 1950; Delilah and the Space-
Rigger, 1949; Space Jockey, 1947; Re-
quiem, 1940; The Long Watch, 1949;
Gentlemen, Be Seated, 1948; The Black
Pits of Luna, 1948; "It's Great to Be
Back!," 1947; "—We Also Walk Dogs,"
1941; Searchlight, 1962; Ordeal in
Space, 1948; The Green Hills of Earth,
1947; Logic of Empire, 1941; The Men-
ace from Earth, 1957; "If This Goes
On—," 1940; Coventry, 1940; Misfit,
1939; Methuselah's Children, 1941)

V. CONSTRUCTION

1. Story Elements

One of the things that every writer runs into, or at least, having accepted the folklore of the writing trade, expects to run into at any time is the fellow who comes up and says, "Listen, I have the greatest ideas. I just don't have the time to write them down. Let's split fifty-fifty. I give you the ideas and you write them and sell them for us." The eternal, inevitable, necessary answer is a hollow laugh, and the reason is that story ideas count for absolutely nothing ninety-nine per cent of the time. Almost anything can prompt a story—a character, a setting, or a situation—but none of these is a story in itself. The idea is nothing, the writing is all. When the story is done, the original idea may or may not even be there.

I hesitate to state categorically what a story *is* because tastes and definitions change. Any definition is a line drawn in the dirt that dares someone to step over it and make you enjoy his doing it. My own idea of a story is the statement of a problem that involves human beings together with a resolution of the problem. The trappings of a story that make it interesting, entertaining, and dramatic are dialogue, characterization, description and details of action. Like any list standing by itself, bare and alone, this is bound to sound bloodless, and it is, in the same way that the list of beef, potatoes, carrots, peas and spices that goes into a stew gives no indication of the hand of the chef in the process and the final flavor of the dish. Writers, like chefs, have their own ways of doing things, and although their stories are made of elements that are similar or identical to the elements of other writers, the stories themselves are marked as individually their own.

In this chapter, I mean to discuss Robert Heinlein's handling of some of the common elements of every story—context, people, problems, and story structure—and his attitude toward his material. The import of the common elements is clear. Every story has a context, a physical and social setting. An exposition of this is important in any story, but particularly important in science fiction since most science fictional contexts are invented ones with which the reader must be made familiar. Since my idea of a story involves human beings, consistent and interesting characters must also be invented and set down as story population. The crux of any story is the central problem which arises from the interaction of people within the story context, and which must be resolved (or, in a gimmick story, illuminated—see "Columbus Was a Dope," for instance) to bring the story to a satisfactory conclusion.

As I'm using the word, structure is the plan of the action of the story. This can generally be represented by a diagram showing the direction of story movement from the opening of the story problem to its resolution. Edgar Rice Burroughs, the creator of Tarzan and John Carter of Mars, for instance, was fond of using a two-pronged structure: that is, he would split his two central characters and follow one until she or he got into a terrific pickle and then cut back to the other and do the same thing again, the cliff-hangers coming at the end of every chapter and the two story lines converging at the climax. The total number of possible plans of action is immense, but most writers seem to prefer to restrict themselves to a favored two or three.

Attitude toward material is tremendously important to the final story. Almost any sort of story—satire, buffoon comedy, melodrama or high tragedy—can be made of the same basic material— the dispossession of a Danish prince, for instance. The difference lies in the attitude of the author to his material, the things he emphasizes and the things he discounts, the complexity or simplicity of the story he makes from the basic material, and his seriousness or lack of seriousness.

These things are half of what makes a writer individually himself. The other half is the words he sets on the page—what he actually does with the materials he has assembled. Included in this are such things as style and dialogue on one hand and on the other the degree to which the writer realizes the potential of the situations, characters and problems he has assembled. But these things will be taken up in the next chapter.

2. Context

Characterizing situations has always been one of Heinlein's strongest points, and I think it is safe to say that he has always done better with developing his societies than he has with developing individual characters. The reason for this seems to lie in Heinlein's engineering interest in how things work. Describing what people do and letting it go at that is not enough to satisfy in fiction. We demand reasons for what people do. Heinlein does give us reasons but he doesn't dwell on them and examine them lovingly. It isn't a thing he cares deeply about and he doesn't labor at the business. On the other hand, telling how a society operates, giving detail, is quite enough to satisfy since nobody is quite sure why even our society is the way it is. Look at the internecine warfare that goes on in the social sciences, and almost any science fiction story that purports to tell *why* things work as they do is bound to seem superficial and less than convincing. Heinlein in general has preferred to show *how* things work in such consistent detail that his societies speak for themselves; they don't need to be explained or justified. Mark Reinsberg, in his introduction to Heinlein's Future History volume, *The Green Hills of Earth*, has written that Heinlein has given the future a daily life, which may be another way of saying the same thing.

Heinlein's most ambitious attempt to create a context is his Future History (newly republished in 1967 in one volume), a body of work that taken as a whole some people consider his most important.

In essence, what Heinlein did was to give a detailed picture of the next two hundred years and a sketchier picture of five hundred years more. This is an amazing and ambitious undertaking involving twenty stories written and rewritten over more than twenty years. Other writers—such as H. Beam Piper, James Blish, Poul Anderson, and Isaac Asimov—have attempted similarly detailed futures in the years since Heinlein began his, and I think that most of them owe credit to Heinlein for scouting the territory for them.

The Future History does not actually form a complete whole. It was not planned as a unit in advance, and it belongs primarily to Heinlein's adolescence as a writer. It was assembled by compromise, chopping, and rewriting. The result is that the individual pieces stand up well enough by themselves while the Future History they supposedly form does not.

The first notice of the Future History came in an editorial note in the March 1941 *Astounding* which pointed out that all of Robert Heinlein's stories up to that time (except for two fantasies published in *Unknown*) were based on common assumptions. In the May 1941 issue, a detailed and involved chart was published that listed the imagined dates of all his Future History stories, the life spans of his various characters, and the technical, sociological and historical outlines of his projected future. Adjustments in the chart were made later and more stories were introduced into it, but what was recognizably the same chart appeared as endpapers in the first four volumes of the Future History to be published in book form, *The Man Who Sold the Moon*, *The Green Hills of Earth*, *Revolt in 2100*, and *Methuselah's Children*, though not in the last volume, *Orphans of the Sky*. A much revised version was published in *The Past Through Tomorrow*, the 1967 omnibus volume.*

The chart covers the period from 1950 to 2600 A.D. In the 1941 chart, there is a break from 1990 until 2070, with one exception, "Logic of Empire," the story about slavery on Venus, which takes place about 2010.

---

* " 'Let There Be Light' " and the unwritten stories have been dropped from the canon, and "Searchlight" and "The Menace from Earth" have been added. There are other changes in the body of the chart.

By the end of 1941, every story which takes place after 2070 in the Future History had been published. These cover the revolt against religious tyranny, the new constitution, the breaking of the constitution, and the exploration of the stars: the stories that appear in *Revolt in 2100*, *Methuselah's Children*, and *Orphans of the Sky*. They do form a whole, except for "Misfit," and I suspect were conceived as a group.

The stories that are set before 2010, on the other hand, do not form a whole and do not really connect with the stories on the other side of the gap. Heinlein continued to add stories to this front part of the Future History until 1962, but he never attempted to bridge the sixty years between 2010 and 2070. Those that come before are near-future speculation; *"If This Goes On—"* is set in a different world with an almost medieval tone.

This gap is one of the two things that reveal the improvised nature of the Future History. The other is the visible chopping and fitting that was carried out through the years.

" 'And He Built a Crooked House,' " the story of the tesseract house, was originally listed in 1941 as a Future History story. It doesn't tie to any of the other stories, however, and was eventually dropped.

" '—We Also Walk Dogs,' " a 1941 Anson MacDonald story, was not originally included in the Future History, but was later rewritten to make it fit. The fit is still an uncomfortable one: the advances that are the subject of the story appear neither in the chart nor in the later stories.

"The Green Hills of Earth" was not originally thought of as a Future History story. There are references to Rhysling and his songs in a definitely non-Future History novel, *Farmer in the Sky*, and Mary Risling of *Methuselah's Children* had to be changed into "Mary Sperling" to make room for this new Rhysling.

"The Long Watch," too, was only finally fitted or shoehorned into the Future History. It derives from Heinlein's juvenile *Space Cadet*, again definitely non-Future History, and in fact is nothing more nor less than an expansion of a paragraph on page 22 of that novel.

Reading straight through the whole Future History isn't even necessary to show its lack of unity. Simply reading *The Green Hills of Earth* from cover to cover is enough to show that this is no more than a collection of stories, some of them quite good ones, that don't happen to have a whole lot to do with one another. As Heinlein himself wrote in a note in *Revolt in 2100*:

> . . . These stories were never meant to be a definitive history of the future (concerning which I know no more than you do), nor are they installments of a long serial (since each is intended to be entirely independent of all the others). They are just stories, meant to amuse and written to buy groceries.

However, if the Future History as written fails to add up to a whole, the chart of the Future History serves as a very impressive example of developing a context, as a close reading of it will show. It is so impressive, in fact, that its existence alone has been enough to lend the impression of connection to a set of stories that would otherwise not have seemed closely related.

More important than this *tour de force* to the question of Heinlein's strengths as a writer is his performance in individual stories. Here, much less flamboyantly, and as his skill grew, much more convincingly, he applied the lessons of his Future History chart rather than those of his Future History.

For some idea of his method, let's take the short story "The Menace from Earth." The core of this story is human beings flying under their own power. Heinlein quite evidently started with this as an idea and wanted to make it plausible, both in itself and as an element in society. A severely reduced gravity, such as that of the Moon, combined with air under normal pressure and elaborate wings solve the problem of possibility. He adds a volcanic bubble underground on the Moon, serving as an air storage tank (its primary purpose, in fact—a shrewd stroke). This provides a physical setting. The social context is the Lunar equivalent of the ski slope, and for this Heinlein has invented rules of the road, learner's wings, flightmasters, and a few other likely possibilities. For added conviction, before Heinlein ever introduces his flying, he shows us the underground nature of Luna City and the low gravity of the Moon in bits of pertinent action.

The heart of Heinlein's technique is the combination of actual fact (the Moon's low gravity) with possible "facts" within the story (the volcanic bubble as air tank). The difference between this and the "facts" on economics, say, that Edward Bellamy presents in *Looking Backward* is that Bellamy presents his facts statically in lectures while Heinlein uses his actively. In this case, we *see* people flying, flying is used as a background within which human problems are developed and come to a conclusion, flying provides a plausible, believable, possible context for people and their problems.

A large part of Heinlein's ability, and a large part of his appeal, lies in the possible but not obvious nature of the trappings of his contexts. Given the actual and the possible, and flying on the Moon follows, but not obviously. Most of us have encountered moments in fiction that carry an emotional shock of recognition. These usually come when there is perfect emotional communication between writer and reader: the writer has his character do, or say, or think, or feel exactly the right thing for the situation, and that thing is so right that although looking ahead it can't be seen coming, looking back it seems inevitable. Heinlein's forte has been not the emotional shock of recognition, but the intellectual shock of recognition.

Set a problem: given the natures of the Moon and Mars, think of a plausible cargo to be carried from a settlement on one to a settlement on the other. The things that come to my mind are obvious and dull—ore of some sort, possibly. Heinlein came up with a good answer in *The Rolling Stones*; looking at it objectively, a beautiful answer: used wide-tired bicycles, to be repainted and refurbished in orbit. A bicycle makes perfect low-gravity transportation, so bicycles are plausible. It is cheaper to send bicycles from the Moon to Mars than from Earth to Mars in terms of fuel cost, so bicycles from the Moon to Mars is plausible. And Heinlein makes a demand for bicycles on Mars plausible by providing two applications for them, prospecting and tourism, the second application invented by the protagonists of the story when the first turns out to be less important than they had thought. To come up with an answer like this requires not only facts about the Moon and Mars, but certain sorts of societies in both places. Heinlein's strength is such that I am quite sure that he could have invented any number of other cargoes, all just as unobvious and just as believable.

The two most central requirements of any context are that it be self-consistent and that it be used. The more complex a context is, the more believable, but also the more difficult to build consistently. The fault of too many science fiction stories of the cheaper variety is that their contexts involve little more than the obvious, the cargo of ore from the Moon to Mars, and the little that isn't obvious— say, the drink of *zlith* that the hero gulps down in the second chapter for a quick lift—comes from nowhere, serves no purpose except to add false color, and thereupon disappears never to be heard of again.

Heinlein has by and large been able to build complex, consistent societies, the complexity coming from individual elements that fit together at the same time that they are used to further the story action. "The Menace from Earth," while a nice little example, is actually minor stuff. One of Heinlein's longer stories, say, *Beyond This Horizon*, provides a much better sample of what Heinlein can do.

The society of *Beyond This Horizon* is tightly planned. It is not threatened from without. Everyone has a basic living wage. Mankind is being gradually improved by the selection of favorable genetic traits. Life in the society is safe and sane for anybody who simply wants to continue living and die at a ripe old age.

This is, of course, the typical utopian dream that as given in a standard manner seems like nothing so much as a vision of eternal boredom. Heinlein has realized this: in fact the problem is implicit throughout the entire story. The people in this society, as people are wont to do, chafe at its strictures. They gamble. They search for thrills. They take to wearing sidearms and invent an involved code of behavior, violations of which lead to duels, simply to keep things lively.

More than this, however, malcontents seek to overturn the society. Revolution is a common theme in science fiction but seldom if ever for such a plausible reason as boredom. In fact, the return to a more primitive life in which there is obvious point is one of the appeals of the revolutionaries. Heinlein, however, rejects this. Revolutions usually settle very little and a return to the simple life is not likely. Heinlein has the revolution defeated as summarily as it would actually be, led as it is by dilettanti. He offers instead an alternative solution: setting to work on some of the larger, less obvious, perhaps impossible-to-solve problems that have kept men awake nights wondering. In other words, Heinlein's answer to a static situation is not to retrench, but to find new goals.

This picture is built consistently and subtly at all points, subtly enough, certainly, that much of the picture I've just given is set down only in background detail and never explicitly stated. For instance, as an indication of stagnancy, Heinlein shows men comparing nail polish. Football, re-introduced, is accepted wildly, but only after it has been beefed up so that deaths are involved. A scientist just back from Pluto is used for effective contrast; his little outpost society is engaged in solving real problems and not in wasting time fighting duels so that he finds himself at something of a loss when expected to carry a gun again. A fading dance star is so anxious to have something to *do* that she undertakes a long jaunt to entertain the outposts on Mars and Pluto. These details are not pounded home—the fingernail polish is used just once and dropped—but they do form a consistent picture. They form a genuine, solid, three-dimensional context.

3. People

Heinlein's characterization has not shown the variety that his contexts have, but in a way this makes very good sense. Basically, Heinlein has used the same general characters in story after story, and has kept these characters limited ones. There is, however, a distinct difference between limitation in characterization and unconvincing characterization. One is neutral and the other is negative, and Heinlein's characterization has always been more neutral than anything else.

One would think that almost every writer in attempting to characterize would describe his people physically, if nothing else, but in actual practice this doesn't hold true. In fact, there are a number of writers, Robert Heinlein among them, who make it a deliberate policy not to describe their characters. Heinlein always gives the sex, sometimes the age, sometimes the size ("tall"), but seldom anything more than this, particularly since his first period.

The policy, as nearly as I can tell, comes from Murray Leinster. The reason for it seems to be that if a character is not described, the reader can picture him as he pleases, and the picture doesn't even have to come close to that held by the writer. In actual practice, the reader usually never notices that the description is not there. He does what Leinster or Heinlein expects and forms his own picture.

Generally speaking, however, I don't think the practice is a very good one. First, while the reader doesn't notice the lack of description while he reads, afterwards individual characters aren't likely to stand out in his mind. Leinster's characters are a blank-faced crowd and Heinlein's characters, with one exception, are not particularly singular. Second, the policy can lead to occasional shocks. For instance, Mr. Kiku, the wily diplomat in *The Star Beast*, turns out to be an old man, but Heinlein doesn't say so until far into the book, though mention of age or gray hair might have been made early. The realization that Kiku is old requires a readjustment of attitude. Too many readjustments can needlessly ruin a story.

Instead of describing them or giving them different speech patterns, Heinlein has generally differentiated his characters in terms of action and dialogue, what they do and what they say. For the most part, his most striking characters come from his earliest period of writing when he did allow himself a certain amount of latitude: Joe-Jim Gregory, the two-headed mutant in *Orphans of the Sky*, for instance, and Harriman, and Waldo, and Lazarus Long. These stand out, however, more for what and who they are than for any great individuality in personality. More recently, there are Hazel Stone and Mr. Kiku, but it is their positions in their stories that make them stand out, rather than their unique natures. By and large, the most truly individual of Heinlein's characters have been the various aliens that have populated a number of his juvenile novels: the Mother Thing from *Have Space Suit—Will Travel*, Willis the Bouncer from *Red Planet*, Lummox from *The Star Beast*, and "Sir Isaac Newton," the Venerian dragon from *Between Planets*, and part of their individuality may come from the fact that they are of necessity more thoroughly described than Heinlein's human characters.

There is one unique and vivid human Heinlein character, but he is a composite of Joe-Jim Gregory, Harriman, Waldo, Lazarus Long, Mr. Kiku and many others, rather than any one individual. I call the composite the Heinlein Individual. In its various avatars it is Heinlein's most serious attempt at characterization. It is a single personality that appears in three different stages and is repeated in every Heinlein book in one form or another.

The earliest stage is that of the competent but naive youngster. The hero of almost any Heinlein juvenile will serve as an example, as will John Lyle of *"If This Goes On—"* and Valentine Michael Smith of *Stranger in a Strange Land*. The second stage is the competent man in full glory, the man who knows how things work. Examples of this are Zeb Jones of *"If This Goes On—,"* the secret-agent narrator of *The Puppet Masters*, and Sergei Greenberg of *The Star Beast*. The last stage is the wise old man who not only knows how things work, but why they work, too. Jubal Harshaw of *Stranger in a Strange Land* is an example, and Baslim of *Citizen of the Galaxy*, and Colonel Dubois of *Starship Troopers*. However, these three stages as I have given them are simply the equivalents of frames cut from a movie film to serve as illustrations—the Heinlein Individual forms a continuum covering all points between youngster and wise old man.

Outside of this Heinlein Individual, there is usually a small supporting cast of side men in any one book. Their most striking feature is their competence, reflecting that of the Heinlein Individual. Beyond that, however, hardly any attempt is made to individualize them, for, after all, they are no more than supporting characters, and if lead characters are not described, what can be expected for less important players? After this small circle, Heinlein ordinarily relies on caricature, and he has a number of set pieces which he produces as needed. One is that of Whining, Useless, Middle-Aged Mama—the mother of John Thomas Stuart in *The Star Beast* is an example. Matching this is the Pompous Male Blowhard—for example, Secretary for Spatial Affairs MacClure, to go again no farther than *The Star Beast*. A third is the Nasty Young Weasel, usually named something like "Sneaky" Weems. You can find examples of him in *Starman Jones, Citizen of the Galaxy*, and *Space Cadet*, among others. Further caricatures could be named, but let's stop with these.

I have only two real criticisms to make of Heinlein's characterization, one of which I have already given—nondescription of characters. The other is Heinlein's lack of ability in drawing convincing women. There is a vast difference, for instance, between Heinlein's standard juvenile hero and Podkayne Fries, or Holly Jones of "The Menace from Earth." Podkayne uses artificial slang, deceives herself regularly, and is less than completely competent—she comes, in fact, closer to being a caricature than she does to being a female example of the Heinlein Individual. Heinlein's adult women generally appear little and then as background figures in all but his third period stories, and the women of that period, Barbara Wells of *Farnham's Freehold*, for example, are little more than voices repeating dialogue, not rounded characters. This lack may be one of the reasons that Heinlein's juveniles as a body are his best work—women are not demanded in them as centrally participating figures.

Heinlein's characters, it seems to me, are clear if not striking, and for his purposes this is probably enough. The one overwhelming reason that I can see for the existence of science fiction is its potential for setting the familiar and the unfamiliar side by side to allow new perspectives. Heinlein has concentrated on developing unfamiliar contexts for his stories; if he were to populate these contexts with wild characters, the result might seem chaotic. On the other hand, the small cast of characters that Heinlein has actually used has not been an intrusion in our view of his contexts. Moreover, this balance of unfamiliar backgrounds and familiar people may well be a considerable factor in Heinlein's noted ability to provide lived-in futures. The futures seem lived-in because we can see people we readily recognize living in them. Since the hardest thing to achieve in science fiction is credibility, Heinlein may very well have been distinctly ahead by keeping his characters restricted.

4. Problems

Characters, background, and story problem are the interlocking essentials of any story. A genuine problem, arising from the nature of the background and characters, is probably the most important of the three because characters or background alone are seldom enough to hold attention, but a real and urgent problem requiring a resolution is enough to keep almost anyone reading.

Science fiction's unlimited canvas offers any number of possibilities for the testing of human beings. The trouble has been that much of modern science fiction has been written by men who freeze in the face of unlimited possibility. The result has been a reliance on trivial situations.

One variety of this tail chasing is the arbitrary problem solved in an arbitrary fashion. Here's an example for you: an urgent reason exists for getting from Point A to Point B. Let's say that everybody on board ship has caught the deadly piffle plague and will die if they don't get to the medical station on Planet Zed. Halfway there, however, the ship's hyperspace navigation device goes on the blink and unless it is repaired, everybody on the ship will die. There's the arbitrary problem for you. Instead of opening a drawer, taking out a spare part, and fixing his bloody machine, the genius hero of the story fashions a new frabismus with his bare hands, two pieces of wire and some bat's blood and single-handedly brings the ship in. End of story, arbitrarily solved.

Almost as bad is the silly sort of adventure story that starts running after the science fictional equivalent of the jeweled idol's eye (smuggled gorph beans) and never stops long enough for us to see that we are chasing a meaningless goal. The quest for "The Egg of the Phoenix" in *Glory Road* is exactly this sort of story problem.

There are some very sharp problems set forth in science fiction. Poul Anderson's "The Man Who Came Early"* is a good short example. It poses a familiar character, a modern soldier, in an unfamiliar context, Viking Iceland. The story problem arises from character and situation: the man thinks and acts wrong; by the

* *Fantasy and Science Fiction*, June 1956.

standards of the time and the place, he isn't a real man. The solution of the problem is the character's death. Whether or not you like its conclusion, the story does examine a portion of what it is to be a human being.

All but a small portion of Robert Heinlein's stories ask similarly serious questions about people and society. This, in fact, is the second of Heinlein's obvious strengths, the first being his ability to portray strange contexts. This isn't a small matter, either—it takes real discernment to develop genuine problems from a given situation and character.

As an example, look at the story "Sky Lift." This story is in fact about the deadly piffle plague, but the difference between the story I outlined above and the one that Heinlein actually wrote is great. In this case, the people with the piffle plague ("Larkin's disease") are on Pluto and medical supplies have to be rushed to them. The crux of the story, however, is nothing so empty as a breakdown in an imaginary device. It is an actual fact that to get from Earth to Pluto in nine days means a constant boost at three-and-a-half gravities, and it is another fact that the human body is not built to take acceleration of that sort for that length of time. Heinlein simply sets as one of his story conditions the necessity to get from Earth to Pluto in nine days. The plague is not the story problem. The problem is the difficulties a man encounters in attempting to function at a necessary job under intolerable conditions that are slowly turning him into a moron. The difference between a problem that involves a broken hyperspace navigation device and a problem that involves a broken human being is an important one that deserves to be more widely recognized in science fiction than it presently is.

Take another example: a society that has turned fact into allegory and a man with an inquiring mind. What does the man do when he finds that everything he has been taught is completely wrong?

Or say that a guild system exists and that you can't get a job unless you belong. What does a young fellow do if the only job he wants is protected by a guild he can't join? The obvious fictional reaction would be that he starts a revolution and throws the blighters out. A dozen science fiction novels at a minimum have done just that, but a revolution obscures the central problem that Heinlein takes the time to examine: what does a person do when every choice he has seems a dead end?

Once it is granted that Heinlein chooses genuine problems to examine, it is interesting to see where he lays his emphases. If a story problem results from the interplay of characters and context, there is still a question as to which side of the interplay is emphasized in the problem. With most writers, the question doesn't arise at all. The story problem is always character-centered. An example of a character-centered story is *Starman Jones*: Max Jones' problem, that of being stymied by a guild system, while no doubt widespread in his society, is here given as a *personal* problem solved in a personal manner. In Heinlein's writing, however, just as his stories have emphasized context more than character, as often as not his story problems have been context-centered. This is not common.

The interest, for instance, in Heinlein's very first story, "Life-Line," is in the effect of an invention on society rather than on any individual person. There is still an interplay of human beings and society, but society is central. The same thing holds true for "Misfit," Heinlein's second story. While Andrew Jackson Libby, the young protagonist, is important, he isn't of central importance. The story problem is the building of a space station, not the metamorphosis of a young boy; the metamorphosis is important only in that it makes the final success of the space station complete.

Beyond This Horizon is centrally concerned not with its individual characters but with the human problems of a perfect society. *The Puppet Masters* is concerned with what happens to a society threatened by an enemy that is totally alien, implacable, and totally bent on subjugating it. We see what happens from the point of view of one man, but the story is not his. Both these stories are context-centered.

The emphasis on context-centered story problems was greater in Heinlein's early stories than it has been since, but even in his more recent fiction there have been strong strains of context-centered problems. In *Have Space Suit—Will Travel* there is the minor problem of refurbishing a used space suit. This reveals little about the hero; it reveals a great deal about space suits, which in the developing context of the story become important. This sort of problem is typical of Heinlein and shows his continuing interest in how things work.

5. Structure

As I've said, it is quite possible to make charts of the structure of stories. There are three simple basic structures, and Heinlein has used them all.

A ⟶ - - - -

The very simplest is the straight line. In this, a problem is set and then resolved, and the process of resolution carries the characters a distance away from the original situation. There are two variants.

A ⟶ B

The first version can be illustrated by *The Rolling Stones*. It is an episodic story with an open end. The problem is one of itchy feet, so Heinlein sets his people wandering. The resolution is made when, after a number of episodes, they accept travel and exploration as a way of life. The ending is not a resting point, but an arrow pointing onward.

The Puppet Masters is an example of the second version. The problem is begun by the landing of parasitic slugs, and is solved by their extermination. The characters have moved from Point A to Point B, and no infinite series of points is implied.

The second structure is the spiral. In this case there is movement again from Point A to Point B, but the points are related. For instance, *Tunnel in the Sky* begins with a boy watching and envying a wagon train guide leading a band of settlers out to start a colony on a new world. It ends with the boy a wagon train guide leading another band of settlers in 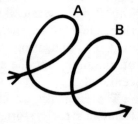 a scene that is a direct replay of the opening scene. A more complicated example is *Glory Road*. Oscar Gordon, the hero, is dissatisfied with life here-and-now. He goes out to find adventure and comes back when the adventure is over to find himself still dissatisfied. In this case, a continuing series of spirals is implied, a series of adventures with stops back at home base in between.

The last structure is the circle. In this one, Point A and Point B are identical. The archetype of this might be the fairy tale in which the protagonist is granted three wishes which he uses badly. The end of the story finds him back in the rude hut from which he started. The structure is used in *Have Space Suit— Will Travel*, and it may be one of the things

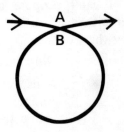

responsible for its fairy tale mood. It might seem at first glance that this is a spiral since the hero comes back from his adventures a wiser, more competent fellow, but it isn't. He comes back to exactly the same point he left, to pick up his life where he left it, back in the drugstore mixing malted milks.

These simple structures can be complicated greatly by various narrative techniques—flashbacks, multiple protagonists, multiple plots, and the like. Generally, however, Heinlein hasn't used them. He has always told his stories in the most straightforward possible manner (and I include "By His Bootstraps" and " 'All You Zombies—' "). The one exception that occurs to me is *Starship Troopers*, which is not related in order. Heinlein has always stuck to one point of view and one protagonist, and any experimentation along these lines (*Beyond This Horizon*, for instance) has been mild.

6. Attitude

The words "romance" and "realism" are very slippery things to take hold of, and will be just as long as we can call Tennessee Williams both a realist and a romantic and mean something by the terms. The dictionary doesn't help greatly, either. *Realism:* "A tendency to face facts and be practical rather than imaginary or visionary; the attempted picturing of people and things as they really are." *Romance:* "A fictitious tale of wonderful and extraordinary events, characterized by much imagination and idealization; a type of novel with emphasis on love, adventure, etc." Where does that put *Robinson Crusoe*, a practical, fact-facing story about wonderful and extraordinary events?

I can't propose a crisp, satisfactory and exhaustive definition of either word, but I can think of different things that I mean by the words:

Romance	Realism
sensitive	not sensitive
simple	complex
subjective	objective
poetic	prosaic
emotional	intellectual
life-not-as-experienced	life-as-experienced
uncritical	critical
sentimental	tough-minded
warm	cold
implausible	plausible
clichéd	unclichéd

It seems to me that any story that could be described by a preponderance of words from one list could then be labeled either romantic or realistic. Let's take an example, a *Saturday Evening Post* story that I remember from the days when I combed old stacks of the *Post* for no reason that I can think of, except perhaps that at thirteen I found them entertaining. In this story, a jealous and protective father and his pretty young daughter live near an airbase. The protagonist is an airman who persuades the daughter to go to a dance with him against her father's wishes. However, they don't get back home on time and the father suspects the worst. When they do arrive, they say they had an auto breakdown on the way home. The father doesn't believe this for a moment and kicks the airman off his place. But then he has second thoughts: the airman was oil top-to-bottom and there wasn't a single paw print on daughter's white party dress. A happy ending follows, the airman being admitted to be a first-class citizen and daughter being allowed to go out with him again. Stretching a point, this situation is life-as-experienced and prosaic. The treatment of the situation, however, is emotional, simple, implausible and clichéd. The situation, then, is realistic, after a fashion. The treatment is romantic.

In the same way, it seems to me that all speculative fiction is bound to be romantic in situation. Science fiction stories are seldom life-as-experienced, seldom prosaic. Some may be closer to what we know or think to be true, or closer to us in space or time than others, and hence more realistic, but this is a relative thing. For a non-reader of science fiction, what is there to choose from between the situation of *The Dragon in the Sea* and that of *The Weapon Shops of Isher*, between "The Cold Equations" and Captain Future, *The Enemy Stars* and *The Dying Earth*? To regular readers of science fiction, there is a difference, but to an outside observer all of these situations are likely to seem equally strange. It seems to me, then, that within science fiction any major distinction between romantic and realistic stories has to be made in terms of treatment.

Heinlein's story situations are sometimes more romantic than their science fictional nature requires. Take, for example, two of Heinlein's accounts of the first trip to the Moon. In one case, *Rocket Ship Galileo*, Heinlein has three boys and a scientist hop off to the Moon in the scientist's private spaceship. In the other, "The Man Who Sold the Moon," the first trip to the Moon is financed by an extinct animal, the old-fashioned entrepreneur of the Carnegie-Rockefeller variety. These situations are thoroughly romantic, and just as romantic are the situations of *Sixth Column* (seven men and super-science throw out a PanAsian invader), *Double Star* (we want *you* to impersonate the Supreme Minister of the Solar System), and *Glory Road* (needed, a Hero), just to name three.

On the other hand, Heinlein's attitude toward his material is with little exception overwhelmingly realistic. It is prosaic, plausible, complex, critical, unsentimental, and life-as-experienced. More important, however, to his realism is the fact that Heinlein's treatments are intellectual rather than emotional. Arthur Jean Cox has pointed out that Heinlein's stories have more warmth than passion, and this is one aspect of Heinlein's intellectualism. Heinlein's characters seldom become angry, seldom become excited, seldom cry, feel despair or elation. Like Heinlein they are interested in facts and in knowing how things work; passion would only be an intrusion in their lives.

An example of this intellectualization can be seen in Heinlein's use of one of the ideas that he lent Theodore Sturgeon in a dry period, the idea that the reading of news may be a cause of mental illness. Heinlein's use is non-dramatic, factual, and general: Jubal Harshaw of *Stranger in a Strange Land* tells one of his secretaries to make a note of the idea so that Harshaw can write an article on the cause of neurosis. Sturgeon's use of the idea in the short story "And Now the News," on the other hand, is dramatic, personal and specific: he is concerned with one man driven insane by a compulsion to identify with other people's troubles. The difference is in attitude. Heinlein's attitude is intellectual, Sturgeon's emotional, and in the same way, Heinlein's stories are always interesting but seldom, if ever, moving.

An added factor in Heinlein's realism is his constant seriousness of purpose. There is no comedy in his stories, or even levity, only a smattering of satire, and very little in the way of pure adventure. Heinlein picks serious problems to write about and solves them as directly as he can.

On balance, then, I would call Heinlein a realist. His situations are romantic, but the difference between a romantic science fiction situation and a realistic one is comparative, and Heinlein's realism in treatment is so pervasive and so marked as to put him definitely in the realistic column.

VI. EXECUTION

1. Stories on Paper

To an extent, any division between the construction and the execution of a story is artificial, just as it is artificial to discuss the context, characters and problems of a story outside their relation to one another. No story exists until it is actually told, and by then construction and execution are so interwoven that a clear separation of them is no longer possible. Still, realizing that the distinction is an artificial one, I'm going to go ahead and make it, mainly because it is convenient. For one thing, it seems to me that the most pertinent criticisms of Heinlein's stories can be made of the things he has done with his basic materials rather than of the materials themselves. As an example, when Heinlein has taken time out in his most recent stories for an irrelevant conversation on sexual morality, the weakness is not in the framework of his story but in the tale built upon the framework.

In this chapter, I will first discuss the words in which Heinlein tells his stories: his style in narrative and dialogue. I suppose that this could be regarded as a part of his basic materials, but it seems to me that there is this difference, that the author's style is not necessary to a particular story in the same manner that a particular person, problem and setting as seen from a particular point of view are; style is a personal embellishment. As an analogy, though the Gothic style of architecture might be basic to an architect, it isn't necessary to his building in the same way that bricks and wood and glass are. Style is always a matter of execution.

Next I'm going to take up Heinlein's handling of sexual relationships in his stories. This has its intrinsic interest, of course, but it seems particularly worth discussing both because Heinlein suddenly started writing about sex after ignoring it for years and because his originality lapses badly whenever he puts a man and a woman in the same bed, or even in the same room.

Heinlein's plotting has probably been the most sharply criticized area of his writing through the years. For instance, Damon Knight said in *In Search of Wonder** that weak plots was one of the two adverse criticisms of Heinlein that he could make (the other was Heinlein's use of slang). Heinlein's plotting is the third major theme of this chapter.

Finally, I mean to abandon the distinction between construction and execution completely and examine three of Heinlein's stories in the light of the points discussed in the last chapter and this one. This time, however, instead of being criticized as examples of fiction in general, as before, the stories will be examined for what they show of Heinlein as an individual writer.

2. Style

Every writer has his own individual way of putting things, his own style. Given a computer and half a dozen factors—average length of word, number of words per paragraph, length of sentences, proportion of various parts of speech to the whole, and so on—identifying any writer should be a simple matter of comparison. The personal stamp of a man is on the things he says and the way that he says them.

Most writers would just as soon have things this way. They write because they want to be heard as individuals. However, some don't

* 2nd ed., p. 77.

sound individual at all to the ordinary reader, which is their personal misfortune. A man who sounds individually himself is going to appeal to more readers than a man who sounds like a thousand other people. I'm not talking, of course, of the man who sounds like himself not because he sees and expresses himself more clearly than other people, but because he is so lacking in powers of observation that nobody else could be quite as bad as he is in his own special way. I'm speaking of writers of ability.

Listen to these two passages, both from heavily sensual writers. First Jack Vance:

> Through the dim forests came Liane the Wayfarer, passing along the shadowed glades with a prancing lightfooted gait. He whistled, he caroled, he was plainly in high spirits. Around his finger he twirled a bit of wrought bronze — a circlet graved with angular crabbed characters, now stained black.*

Then Ray Bradbury:

> It had been raining for seven years; thousands upon thousands of days compounded and filled from one end to the other with rain, with the drum and gush of water, with the sweet crystal fall of showers and the concussion of storms so heavy they were tidal waves come over the islands. A thousand forests had been crushed under the rain and grown up a thousand times to be crushed again. And this was the way life was forever on the planet Venus, and this was the school room of the children of the rocket men and women who had come to a raining world to set up civilization and live out their lives.†

For all the sensuality they have in common, these are distinctly different writers. I don't see how a page from one could possibly be mistaken for a page from the other.

A goodly portion of what makes style is bound up in the devices a writer chooses to make his work vivid. For instance, Poul Anderson says of a policy that he follows: "A useful device—I think it was first enunciated by Flaubert—is to invoke at least three senses in every scene, remembering that we have much more than five senses."**

* *The Dying Earth*, Hillman Periodicals, Inc., New York, 1950, p. 71.
† "All Summer in a Day," *Fantasy and Science Fiction*, March 1954.
** Personal letter.

In the opening scene of Anderson's Hugo-winning novelette, "No Truce With Kings,"* there are the following bits of sensual data: shouts, stamping boots, the thump of fists on tables, clashing cups, shadows, stirring banners, winking light, wind and rain outside, a loosened collar, singing, a chill feeling, a dark passageway, and clattering footsteps—all of these and others in a matter of six hundred words or so. They tie you to what is happening. This is not a bad policy, but neither is it an easy one to follow, mainly because no matter what a writer may determine to set down, what he actually puts on paper is not completely controlled by his conscious mind. This policy is also, as Anderson says, not the only solution to the problem of making writing real and vivid.

Theodore Sturgeon has a good sense of the nuances of speech and of shades of meaning. He draws delicate portraits. This, I think, is the key to his work: he draws word portraits. His writing, even to his similes and metaphors, is visually oriented. He has the artist's eye and it marks his work as something different than Vance's, or Bradbury's, or Anderson's:

> The idiot lived in a black and gray world, punctuated by the white lightning of hunger and the flickering of fear. His clothes were old and many-windowed. Here peeped a shinbone, sharp as a cold chisel, and there in the torn coat were ribs like the fingers of a fist. He was tall and flat. His eyes were calm and his face was dead.†

The common element that links Vance, Bradbury, Anderson, and Sturgeon is their use of sense impressions to make their writing vivid. Robert Heinlein, however, is an almost extreme opposite. His writing is not sensual in any degree. Instead, he depends on other things—description of people and things in action, and clever turns of phrase—to catch and hold attention.

No matter what policy he would like to follow, a writer in practice tells what he sees. The impressions that are important to him are the ones he passes on. Sturgeon lingers over visual impressions. Anderson ticks them off and then goes on to record thumps, clashes and the feel of a loosened collar. Heinlein gives only a minimum of visual

---

* *Fantasy and Science Fiction*, June 1963.

† *More Than Human*, Farrar, Straus & Young, New York, 1953, p. 3.

description, and never lingers with it at all, and gives even less of other sensual impressions.

In speaking of Heinlein's characterization, I mentioned that he hardly bothers with the looks of his characters. Here are the three secretaries of Jubal Harshaw in *Stranger in a Strange Land*:

> Anne was blonde, Miriam red-headed, and Dorcas dark; they ranged, respectively, from pleasantly plump to deliciously slender. Their ages spread over fifteen years but it was hard to tell which was the eldest.

(It also seems difficult to keep them separate, since this is all the description you ever get of these moderately important characters.)

Heinlein's backgrounds, for all that they are well-developed, are also featureless. *Glory Road*, an open-air adventure much like the Vance story quoted above is *sans* color, *sans* sights, *sans* sounds. Rooms, landscapes, cities—microcosm to macrocosm—all in Heinlein are given only in outline, never in detail.

Even so, Heinlein's writing *is* vivid. His solutions are simply different. Since his continuing interest is in process—how things both physical and social work—Heinlein doesn't tell what things look like, he tells what they *do*. For an example, in *Beyond This Horizon*, Heinlein has one of his characters introduce a Colt .45 automatic. Physically, it is "novel," "odd," "uncouth," and has a stud on its side which when pressed lets a long, flat container slide out. That's it. That's all you get. If you had never seen a .45 automatic, you would be no better off for Heinlein's description of it. You might mistake it for a gum machine (novel, odd, uncouth; has a stud on its side which when pressed lets a long, flat container—your gum—slide out). On the other hand, in dialogue Heinlein lets us know more about it and he demonstrates how it works very nicely. You still don't know what the damned thing looks like, but you know very well what it does.

" 'Value' "—says Colonel Dubois of *Starship Troopers*—"has two factors for a human being: first, what he can do with a thing, its *use* to him . . . and second, what he must do to get it, its *cost* to him." This is very much Heinlein's attitude in writing. He wants to work out how his characters can use a thing and what it will cost them.

He doesn't really care whether it looks like a gum machine or a .45 automatic. He wants to know if you have to put a nickel into it before the long, flat container slides out, and whether what you get is a magazine of bullets or a pack of gum. This is not a bad attitude to have in writing science fiction where so much encountered is strange. Does it matter what the monster looks like? The question is whether or not he bites. Does it matter what the machine looks like? The question is whether or not it works. Does it matter what the character looks like? The question—for Heinlein in particular— is whether or not he is capable of doing the right thing at the proper moment.

Of course, it does matter what these things look like. Not described at all, they become tricks produced from a hat. Some description is always necessary. Beyond minimum description, however, definition by demonstration can be effective. Properly speaking, it isn't an abandonment of detail, but the choice of a different sort of detail to report.

Heinlein relies heavily on clever phrasing to carry his stories. He has an ear for brisk, bright metaphor. In his early writing, this brightness appeared more in narrative than in dialogue. Here is a description of a situation from *Beyond This Horizon*:

> The poor degenerate starveling descendants of the once-mighty Builders of Mars can hardly be described as intelligent—except in charity. A half-witted dog could cheat them at cards.

Heinlein does not have a particularly acute ear for individualities of speech—his characters have always sounded very much alike. In his early stories, at most one character was blessed with the ability to speak in brisk, bright, clever metaphor. The rest spoke a simple, utilitarian English. The one character (usually a Heinlein Individual of the competent or wise old man stage) was thus enabled to stand out a bit from the crowd:

> "Well, it could be that she simply became shocked at over-hearing a rather worldly and cynical discussion between the Holy One and, oh, say the High Bursar—taxes and tithes and the best way to squeeze them out of the peasants. It might be something

like that, although the scribe for such a conference would hardly be a grass-green Virgin on her first service." (*"If This Goes On—"*)

"You broke? Shucks, I've been there myself. Relax." The man waggled his fingers at the waitress. "Come here, honey chile. My partner and I will each have a breakfast steak with a fried egg sitting on top and this and that on the side. I want that egg to be just barely dead. If it is cooked solid, I'll nail it to the wall as a warning to others." (*Starman Jones*)

"Uh, Star, I've got a still better idea. Why don't we high-tail it back the way we came and homestead that spot where we caught the fish? In five years we'll have a nice little farm. In ten years, after the word gets around, we'll have a nice little motel, too, with a free-form swimming pool and a putting green." (*Glory Road*)

There is enough of a cumulative effect in both narrative and dialogue that Heinlein's writing soon becomes easily recognizable. Unfortunately, however, in Heinlein's third-period stories there has been a three-fold change. There are now more characters using brisk, bright metaphor in dialogue, those characters speak pithily more often, and the total amount of dialogue in Heinlein's stories has increased. This is not good, first because stories need action to carry them along, not static campfire pow-wows, and second because the more one hears of people who all talk in the same unusual way, the less individual they become. Brisk, bright cleverness in narrative is acceptable since it can be taken as the author's personal style. As dialogue, it seems mannered and artificial. This may be a contributing factor in the falling off in quality of Heinlein's most recent stories.

3. Sexual Relationships

There was a story some years ago by Walter M. Miller, Jr. and Lincoln Boone about a particularly unpleasant comedian named Martin Snyder.* Snyder had a trademark—at the punchline of one of his jokes he would remove a monocle he wore, breathe on it, and then polish it while the audience laughed. One night, just to

* "The Corpse in Your Bed Is Me," *Venture Science Fiction*, May 1957.

demonstrate the control he had over his audience, and to justify his contempt for it, he removed the monocle without saying anything, breathed on it, and polished it. He still got his laugh. The comedian was given as thinking of this as a case of conditioned response, but I don't think it was. It strikes me as a case of basic communication.

Communication is a process of symbolization: a person codes a message in such a way that his meaning can be understood by someone else. I speak in a code called English, for instance, and write English in a Latin alphabet. A request for a hamburger in Swahili in the average American restaurant would do me little good, and a message in Braille—for all that it is written in English—would hardly be enough to persuade the milkman to leave me an extra bottle of milk. Communication is an art. Some people are more adept at coding and uncoding messages than others. However, the basis of communication is always in terms of symbols held in common.

In the case of the comedian, Snyder, that removal of the monocle was a common symbol signalling something funny. When the monocle was removed with no joke, this was unexpected and funny— the monocle changed from a signal to something funny in itself. If the laughter had been a conditioned response, the people would have laughed as often as Snyder yanked the monocle out of his eye, whereas I rather think that if he had done it twice without a joke he would have lost his audience.

Our culture is filled with symbols that are held in common as part of our tradition, some of which are hidden so deeply that they are not even widely understood, but merely felt, as for instance the ritual cannibalism in our Christian churches. Some symbols are dead, though still observed generally, like walking on the gutter side of a lady or the ritual of hat-tipping. Some are still alive and full of meaning.

These symbols, both alive and dead, appear in fiction. Any good writer always deals in terms of symbols. The search for the *right* word is no more than the search for a proper and effective symbol. The difference between a good writer and a bad one can be described, I think, in the respective percentages of live and dead symbols they use. We can no longer accept "close-set criminal eyes" as a live symbol of a man's character, for instance, and a writer who sticks close-set criminal eyes into a story is likely to be a bad writer. A good writer finds fresh ways of handling symbols, rather than presenting us with old symbols preserved like ants in amber.

In general, through his career, Robert Heinlein has used and presented ideas freshly, but there is one whole area of his fiction in which he has never used anything but long-dead symbols. I'm speaking of his treatment of sex. In more than seventy stories Heinlein has presented uncoy, unclichéd inter-sexual relations no more than twice, the two cases being thoroughly married couples in "The Unpleasant Profession of Jonathan Hoag" and "It's Great to Be Back." I suspect that Heinlein isn't comfortable with the subject.

At first glance, it would seem that Heinlein almost completely ignored sex for years, mentioning it only when he had to and then obliquely, and then in his third period became obsessed by it, making a complete about-face. There is some truth in this, but in actual fact the old Heinlein and the new one are not as separate as that first glance makes them seem to be.

The first Heinlein story with a major female character was *"If This Goes On—."* In the original version, the hero, John Lyle, falls in love at first sight with a sweet, young, innocent, professional Virgin. Damon Knight quite accurately calls it a "story-book romance"*— a tag for the sort of dead symbolism I'm trying to point to. With the romance established, Heinlein (and apparently Lyle, too) forgets about the girl until the end of the story when she and her marriage to Lyle are mentioned in passing.

In the expanded version of the novel, Heinlein tried to make Lyle's relationships more likely. He replaced the story-book romance with another involving Lyle and a different handmaiden of the Prophet. The odd thing is that the new romance is right out of a story-book, too.

In both versions, Lyle is naive, but his naiveté is more obvious in the expanded story, partly because the added length gives him more of an opportunity to display himself. Everybody else knows that there are all sorts of backstairs assignations going on in the Palace.

* *In Search of Wonder*, 2nd ed., p. 77.

Lyle doesn't. Zeb Jones, Lyle and two girls go on a nude swimming party. Lyle objects when he finds out what he is involved in. Zeb takes one of the two girls off to a private beach and until he is restrained, Lyle wants to go join them . . .

The heroine of the new version is as much a stock character as the heroine of the original. This new one is the Good Bad Girl. She is one of the Prophet's sexual castoffs, is Zeb's ex-mistress, and has slept around. In a scene rewritten and used again as recently as *Glory Road*, she offers her fair body to the hero on a sleep-in basis and then becomes flustered when he insists on marriage first. In this case, the last you see of Lyle and his love together is in a story-book pose: "We had a twenty-minute honeymoon, holding hands on the fire escape outside my office . . ." This is typical of Heinlein's representations of inter-sexual relations. His heroes are pure and never have sex without marriage even when women offer themselves openly—and Heinlein adds purity insurance by making all his young heroes sexually naive.

Also typical of Heinlein is the banter he assigns the central characters in " 'Let There Be Light,' " the second of his stories to include a central female character. The hero and his girl are represented as being scientists at the very top of their respective fields. However, they spend their time calling each other "kid," "mama," "ape," "lug," "sister," "wench," "chum," and "son." When the hero actually gets up the nerve to kiss the girl, she pushes him away, saying, "Archie, you remind me of the Al G. Barnes Circus; 'Every Act an Animal Act.' " The banter and shying around covers acute discomfort, and I suspect the discomfort belongs to Heinlein as much as to his characters.

There are two romances in *Beyond This Horizon.* One is a case of mutual love at first sight (harking back to *"If This Goes On—"*). In the other, the two call each other "Filthy" and "Flutterbrain," and the boy has to get into a physical fight with the girl as an excuse to touch and kiss her for the first time.

By the time of *The Puppet Masters*, there is some advance: neither the hero nor heroine is naive. But the advance is limited. The girl invites the hero to her apartment, mentioning her bed in the invitation, and then locks her bedroom door. The hero sleeps on the living-room couch. Before they sleep together, they get themselves so firmly, tightly married that the marriage clerk finds their contract something to comment on.

In Heinlein's juvenile novels, there are a number of sympathetically drawn marriages, but always between adults, always long-established, always seen at a distance. The marriages are given as facts, not as processes being established. In view of all the other processes Heinlein has written about, this can only seem strange.

The central characters of the juvenile novels are always protected from the facts of life by their naiveté. The hero of *Tunnel in the Sky*, for instance, is pure and ignorant. The people around him are all getting married and having children but not the hero. He quite literally can't even recognize a girl as a girl even when he meets one. His best friend comes out of an extended period of delirium, and Rod, the hero (why Rod?—it doesn't seem appropriate somehow), introduces him to another person approximately as follows:

"Meet my friend Jack with whom I've been in close contact for, lo, these many moons. He's a good boy."

Delirious friend, raising head from pillow: "Boy? You nut—Jack is a girl."

Rod (wonderingly): "Gosh. Are you certain?"

This business is Heinlein's own choice. It is not imposed by story requirements nor even by the fact that the book is a juvenile. Heinlein simply raises sex as a subject and then has his hero blind to it and uninvolved.

Citizen of the Galaxy offers even more reason for wonder. The hero is an ex-slave, ex-beggar, raised in a gutter environment, exactly the sort of person one would think would be sexually knowledgeable if not sexually experienced. However, on two separate occasions in the story he is pursued by attractive girls so openly that everybody else realizes what is going on, and in neither case can he see beyond the end of his nose.

The Door Into Summer dates from the end of Heinlein's middle period, after he had been writing for more than fifteen years; it is not a juvenile. The romantic situation in this story is a very interesting, very odd one: it is nothing less than a mutual sexual interest between an engineer of thirty and a girl of twelve ("adorable" is Heinlein's word for her), that culminates in marriage after some hop-scotching around in time to adjust their ages a bit. It puts me in mind of the popular singer, Jerry Lee Lewis, who married an eleven-year-old girl, saying (if memory serves), "She may be young, but she's all woman."

It seems to me that the sum of the examples I have given so far, typical of Heinlein before his third period, is that all are naive, sentimental, clichéd, uncritical, implausible, and life-not-as-experienced. I would say they were the result of an internalization of romantic ideals that we mouth but don't really observe.

The supreme popular example of the romantic idealist in our culture is the Boy Scout. When I was a Boy Scout, we spent a good deal of time on camping trips, and each night of each camping trip we would lie awake in our tents and tell filthy stories. In the last ten years I haven't heard one-tenth, or even one-fiftieth, of the filthy stories that I heard and told in two years of Scout activity. Those stories are a normal reaction. They are a way of saying that you're really grown-up, that you're a *man* — an analogue of the secret cigaret. They are a way of saying that for all you are a Boy Scout you really know what is going on. And they are daring.

These stories all seemed to rely on wild props: watermelons, Chinese bells, sledgehammers, flashlights and motorcycles. It was one of their two common elements, the other being impossible exaggeration, otherwise known as plain unlikelihood.

In 1959, in " 'All You Zombies—,' " Heinlein wrote a story about sex. It amounts to a boy seducing himself and getting himself pregnant, with a time machine for a wild prop. And not only did Heinlein get the story printed, but it has been reprinted, too. It's a dirty joke—fun, daring, and it shows the whole world that Heinlein really knows what is going on. Since then, *Stranger in a Strange Land*, *Glory Road*, *Farnham's Freehold*, and *The Moon Is a Harsh Mistress* have been offered as additional proof to an unbelieving world that Heinlein really does know what is going on. But a Boy Scout is no less the romantic idealist for his dirty jokes, and neither is Heinlein.

Stranger in a Strange Land is a particularly difficult book to discuss because it is so long, so complicated, and about so many different things. Sex is not treated as a single subject, but as an adjunct to Heinlein's religion. So far as the way the story is constructed goes, the sexual relations are beyond criticism, self-justified. Within the story, anyone incapable of accepting the religion along with its sexual concomitants is not a *real* person; anybody capable of accepting the religion (or, more properly, being accepted by the religion) is automatically beyond damage. This sort of built-in self-protection for the author is no more than a way of writing around a subject without ever coming to grips with it.

I have added reason for this opinion. In none of the four novels named above does Heinlein describe sexual relations directly. There are no textures, no actions, no movements, no thoughts and no feelings. Everything is given in terms of the particularly noxious and limited "Yes, *now*" school of dialogue. It seems a case of deliberately blinding oneself to avoid *seeing* what is being set on paper.

A more central criticism of *Stranger in a Strange Land* is that in the real world, as in the Oneida Community which lacked the protection of a defined-as-right religion, what Heinlein has given is an unstable way of living. Heinlein ignores completely the pain, jealousy and uncertainty that are the ordinary stuff of human experience. He describes a romantic ideal, unworkable in practice. A similar state of affairs exists in *The Moon Is a Harsh Mistress*. Heinlein describes ideal mass marriages as being necessary on the Moon, the result of a population imbalance that several generations have not righted. (One wonders why.) The marriages are odd enough to arouse Kentucky prejudices, but newcomers to the Moon find them instantly acceptable. (One wonders how.) But Heinlein says it works and nobody seems to be anxious, hurt or unhappy.

The situation of *Glory Road* is much simpler. The hero, Evelyn Cyril Gordon, will go to bed with anybody, or so he says. But then he finds excuses. Not with those Vietnamese; they're too childlike (incredible after *The Door Into Summer*; incredible to anybody who has seen a Vietnamese girl). Not with the old girl friend who sent him off to the wars in the traditional way—he assures us it isn't because she is married now; he just doesn't feel like it, that's all. And the heroine, the Empress of the Twenty Universes, she, too, will go to bed with anybody, but when the moment of truth for her and for Heinlein comes she has this convenient wound in her side and just isn't up to it.

Evelyn Cyril is as naive as any former Heinlein hero, any statement in the book to the contrary notwithstanding. It might be claimed for him on other evidence than his sexual oddities that he isn't even half-bright, but I am willing to give him the benefit of the doubt and call him simply another Boy Scout. Just as in *"If This Goes On—,"* when the hero's True Love indicates her willingness and points to a clump of grass (I mean this literally), the hero insists on marriage as his price for submitting.

Glory Road is in some ways the Boy Scout's dream. Imagine waking on a beach to find a beautiful naked girl standing and pointing—"You, you clod, you're the only man for me." But the Boy Scout wouldn't know what to do with his dream if he had it, and Evelyn Cyril's reaction is to stammer of marriage. The difference between an old Heinlein hero and this new one is that Evelyn wears a badge saying, "I'm really not so pure." Only he is.

Farnham of *Farnham's Freehold* does sleep with the heroine the first time he meets her, which seems a departure, but Heinlein can only let him do it by having Farnham reject both his wife and the pretty little bedwarmer he is assigned by his owner when he becomes a slave. Beyond this, the conventions remain as tired and unexamined as ever. Heinlein's married couples are not notably fruitful, but in *Farnham's Freehold*, as in " 'All You Zombies—,' " conception is the result of one isolated night of love; on that basis, you would think Heinlein's juvenile heroes would have many more brothers and sisters than they do.

The point, of course, is that once Heinlein gets even one inch away from a direct concern with men and women together, his maturity, realism and ability to think re-assert themselves. As an example, in *Methuselah's Children* there is a situation that L. Sprague de Camp describes as follows: "the long-lived hero is confronted with the problem of whether to marry his great-great-great-great-grand-daughter.

Genetically their relationship is negligible, but such a union still seems somehow incestuous and wrong."* De Camp is mistaken, however. The union seems incestuous and wrong *only* to the hero, not to the other characters, and not to Heinlein: " 'I know I'm old-fashioned,' he said uncomfortably, 'but I soaked up some of my ideas a long time ago. Genetics or no genetics, I just wouldn't feel *right* marrying one of my own grandchildren.' " In *Time for the Stars*, as though to demonstrate the exact limits of his ability to look at men and women together (and to refute de Camp) Heinlein has his hero come home from journeying among the stars to quite happily fall in love, at first meeting, of course, with his great-grand-niece and marry her.

4. Plot

Heinlein's plotting has probably been the most continually criticized element in his writing, and to me there seems to be justice in the criticism. In fact, we use the word "plot" to cover a multitude of things, and Heinlein has had his problems with at least two of them.

The thing that is usually meant by the word "plot" is the plan of action of a story, the thing that I discussed earlier as "structure." Heinlein had his problems with this when he first started writing. Stories like "Life-Line," "Misfit," "Elsewhen" and *"If This Goes On—"* are severely flawed because they aren't told crisply. They begin with an end in mind and eventually get there, but the route they take is a wandering one. Overcoming this is in part a matter of deciding what the story is really about and learning to pick only significant details, and in part a matter of planning in advance.

By the end of his first period, Heinlein was no longer troubled by this kind of plot weakness, as "By His Bootstraps" amply demonstrates. A man who couldn't plan the structure of a story could not have written "By His Bootstraps," " 'All You Zombies—,' " or *The Door Into Summer*, to name just three that are extremely involved but which do take the shortest routes to their destinations.

However, by the end of his first period, another and very different

* *Science-Fiction Handbook*, p. 225.

sort of "plot weakness" had become apparent in Heinlein's writing. This was not a failure in structure but a failure in providing all the details that the structure demands. Boucher and McComas, for instance, had this to say in reviewing "Waldo": ". . . 'Waldo,' while being his best concept, illustrates the basic weakness in most of Heinlein's work, a tendency to rush the ending and to shirk final developments."* The failure, in other words, is one of execution, not of plot structure *per se*.

This has been a continuing problem with Heinlein. It hasn't been present in every story, but it has been present often enough to make it obvious that Heinlein, if he doesn't keep close control, can let his stories trail away, in de Camp's words, "as if the author had simply grown tired."†

In "Gulf," for instance, Heinlein spends one day in time and thirty-six pages in enrolling an agent. He then spends six months, skimmed over in another thirty-odd pages, in training the agent. Then, just to end the story, he kills his agent off in a job that takes him one day, buzzed over in a mere four pages. The gradual loss of control is obvious.

Farmer in the Sky begins in close focus and then gradually slips away until large amounts of time are covered in sentences. Heinlein then tries to recover his story with a large chunk of closely detailed action. The same thing exactly is true of *Between Planets*, and true again of *Time for the Stars*.

As another aspect of this same problem, Heinlein has also tried to force his stories to go on farther than their plots will carry them. *Beyond This Horizon* is one example, but since the extra words are spent on a very interesting society in action, the flaw is a minor one. *Glory Road* is another example; and since the extra words are spent mainly in discussing the theory of sexual and political morality, the flaw is more than the book can stand.

If Heinlein were consistently troubled by his plots, he would be relatively easy to discuss and to sum up, but the trouble is that he has shown such a wide variance in his plots that he becomes very

---

* *Fantasy and Science Fiction*, Summer 1950.
† *Science-Fiction Handbook*, p. 155.

difficult to categorize. On the one hand there is a story like *Podkayne of Mars* that comes dangerously close to being without any structure at all, let alone a flawed one, and on the other there is a story like *Starman Jones* that is more than adequately built and one like *Have Space Suit—Will Travel* that is beautifully built. The only thing that I can say is that given a Heinlein story and asked to guess before reading it what its most serious problem might be, I would guess that Heinlein had had some trouble with his plot. And about sixty per cent of the time I would be wrong.

5. Some Examples

In this section, I intend to briefly discuss three of Heinlein's stories, "Coventry," *Have Space Suit—Will Travel*, and *Farnham's Freehold*, one from each of his three periods, in light of what I have said about Heinlein's construction and execution.

The context of "Coventry" is the libertarian society developed in the last half of the Future History. One of the advantages of using a general background in several stories is that a complicated context can be given in a short length without need for great explanation. Having established his new society in *"If This Goes On—,"* Heinlein is here free to treat it as a given and then show what happens to those who are unwilling to accept it. He has them placed in an area kept separate by a force field and left to themselves, and allows that any man who cares to can rejoin the United States by acceptance of its social contract.

There are only two developed characters in the story, both aspects of the Heinlein Individual. One is the protagonist, David MacKinnon, a literary critic who answers criticism of himself with punches in the nose, and who is sent to Coventry when he refuses psychological treatment. The other is an agent of the United States operating secretly in Coventry who takes MacKinnon under his wing and keeps him out of trouble. MacKinnon is the naive young Heinlein Individual. The agent is the slightly older, more knowledgeable and more cynical version.

There are two story problems. One arises primarily from the context of the story, and the other primarily from the nature of the protagonist. The contextual problem is how to warn the United States of a planned breakout by the dissident little states within Coventry. The other problem is the rehabilitation of MacKinnon. Unfortunately, Heinlein solves this second problem twice. He does it once by demonstrating to MacKinnon that the sort of rugged individualism he dreams of just doesn't exist, and that for better or for worse he is a member of society. He shows that even the crippled personalities within Coventry find government necessary and that their government is a mess because of their sickness. However, Heinlein then gives MacKinnon a flamboyant chance to demonstrate his new self by sending him off to warn the United States of the potential revolt.

Since Heinlein's two problems are not really closely related, his structure is a divided one and he has to close with an attempt to pull them together. This he does by MacKinnon's flamboyant gesture. This isn't quite satisfactory, however, because Heinlein's realism insists that the potential revolution cannot be a serious threat, that the United States government would be well aware of the situation, and that therefore MacKinnon's journey is not as important as he believed it was. He refocuses attention on MacKinnon's rehabilitation by throwing away the revolution, but the cost of the adjustment is that the rehabilitation seems like an anticlimax.

There is a mild romantic interest, lightly sketched, in which MacKinnon moons after a fifteen-year-old girl, but little is made of this. The story itself is told briskly and straightforwardly. What clever wisecracks are included are restricted to the appropriate character— the middle-stage Heinlein Individual secret agent.

In sum, the context of the story and the problem of the would-be anarchist are the best things about "Coventry." Heinlein's biggest problem is in deciding what the story is really about—in other words, plot structure.

The framing context of *Have Space Suit—Will Travel* is a near-future Earth in which there is a human colony on the Moon but in which hot rods, malted milks, soap slogan contests, and high schools with empty curricula still figure. The story begins with this and returns to it at the end, and it puts parentheses around the novel, but Heinlein concerns himself with a larger context, too, a confederation that unites various races throughout this galaxy and the Magellanic Clouds.

There are three central characters in the story. One is the Mother Thing, perhaps the most charming of Heinlein's aliens, and a representative of the confederation. Heinlein characterizes her as "the cop on the beat," the epitomal policeman. The second is an eleven-year-old female genius, perhaps a little too knowing to be quite believable, but good fun. The third is the narrator, a typical young example of the Heinlein Individual, though not as naive as some. The rest of the characters are background figures, either competents or caricatures.

The main story problem is really handled quite subtly. It is, in fact, nothing less than the determination of the nature of the contact between Earth and the confederation, something to be settled by the thoughts and actions of the little genius and the narrator. Stated flatly, this would be just too much to swallow, but Heinlein leads up to it by very neatly misdirecting his readers with immediate problems and adventures that only in retrospect are seen to be necessary predicates to the central problem.

The story is beautifully plotted. Starting from a mundane tomorrow morning, Heinlein begins a series of little adventures, each one carrying the characters a little farther from that mundane tomorrow, until hardly knowing how one has gotten there, one is set face to face with the confederation and accepts it. The structure on which this plot is built, returning full circle to exactly the point at which it left Earth, is very neatly done, too.

There is a hint of romantic interest to come between the little genius and the hero, but it is again very mildly stated, just as one might expect.

Heinlein's taste for the pithy remark is confined for the most part to description; not inappropriate since his narrator is a Heinlein Individual.

> . . . I was like the Army mule at West Point: an honorary member
> of the student body but not prepared for the curriculum.

> . . . We lived like that "Happy Family" you sometimes see in
> traveling zoos: a lion caged with a lamb. It is a startling exhibit
> but the lamb has to be replaced frequently.

At times, of course, it does sound more sophisticated than might
be expected from an eighteen-year-old boy, but that is a minor point.

In *Have Space Suit—Will Travel*, there is probably as close to an
even balance between characters and background as Heinlein has
ever managed. Though the continuing import of the background is
greater, the import of the characters within the story is re-emphasized.
by the return to Earth and to the original context. The story is theirs.
What comes after belongs to the context.

One of the major flaws of *Farnham's Freehold* is that (unusually
for Heinlein) it lacks a clearly-defined context. The present-day
world is destroyed by bombs by the end of the second chapter. The
woodsy-idyll context is shown to be an illusion. The slave society
to which the characters are taken is not seen in detail; all that is seen
is one portion of one household. This leaves very little for the main
characters to function against.

Only one character is dwelt on at length and that is Farnham
himself. He is a Heinlein Individual somewhere in between the stage
that knows what-is-what and the stage that knows why. Strangely,
however, his competence is questionable, for all that Heinlein asserts
its presence.

There is no story problem in *Farnham's Freehold* except that of
mere survival: survival of the bombs, survival in the woods, survival
in a slave society, survival of the aftermath of the bombs when
Farnham and his wife return to their own time. For some reason,
Heinlein has always regarded sheer survival, as a thing in itself regard-
less of any other factors, as a comforting and sufficient end. Farnham's survival, however, is an accident and nothing that he himself
causes and so on an overt level the story seems pointless.

Part of the problem, of course, is that Heinlein uses the better part
of his space in formal little debates on the subjects of freedom and
race and family relations, and these tangential things substitute for
the story instead of adding to it.

However, if one wants to carry a search for meaning in *Farnham's Freehold* beyond the overt level, another idea of context and story problem does emerge. If the context of the story is really an unheeding universe that treats Farnham like a bemused boy toying with a grasshopper and making it "spit tobacco," then Farnham's futility takes on new meaning. The story may be Heinlein's unconscious way of saying that competence is not enough. The point of the story then becomes the persistent attempt by Farnham to escape from whatever it is that is mistreating him so casually and to find a haven for himself.

In fact, the book may even be taken as the search of a solipsist for a universe in which to be God. If this seems far-fetched, perhaps the following chapter will make it seem less so.

VII. CONTENT

1. Speculation

I'd like to draw a distinction I think is useful between *extrapolation* and *speculation*. Ordinarily the terms are used more or less as equivalents and to a certain extent they necessarily overlap. I think they can be used, however, to distinguish between two different things that go on in science fiction. One is the closely reasoned inferential process. This is extrapolation, an account of the operation of known processes. The other is the less confined concern with how and of what the world is made. This is speculation, an account of the essential nature of things.

There are science fiction stories that obviously lay emphasis chiefly on one or the other of these. Clement's *Mission of Gravity*, for instance, is basically extrapolative. Blish's *The Triumph of Time*, with its human-directed rebirth of the universe, is basically speculative.

Heinlein, of course, is best known as an extrapolator. Nonetheless, he has written speculative stories—"Waldo," for instance—and included bits of mysticism in many more.

There is also a deeper and less obvious sort of speculation in any author's stories. Basically, it could be called the author's attitude toward life, or his conception of the world.

Almost any story has an obvious surface meaning revealed in

action. Hamlet, for instance, is a prince whose uncle has him murdered when the uncle discovers that his crimes have been found out, except that Hamlet is able to take all the bad guys with him when he goes. Beneath the surface of *Hamlet*, however, are other meanings, both reasonably accessible and hidden, and it is these that give the story, and other complex fiction, more interest for a reader than is held by, say, a Nancy Drew thriller or the Bobbsey Twins. These additional meanings illuminate the obvious surface. The bodies on the stage at the end of *Hamlet* are more than just a way of keeping score so that the spectator can see which side came out ahead. A writer's attitude toward life, as much as it can be determined, helps in the same way to illuminate the obvious surface of his fiction.

Meaning that was consciously intended by the writer generally is accessible on one or two readings. A character named Gradgrind points a direction. So does the color of a white whale. The determination of unconscious meanings and of attitudes is more difficult and much less certain. These are never absolutely "provable"; at best they are tentative constructions, useful only to the extent to which they do illuminate—and this may vary from reader to reader. The only method that I know of arriving at these meanings and attitudes is through an examination of those symbols, themes and ideas that a writer chooses to keep repeating beyond any outside necessity.

In this chapter, I intend to discuss two repeated Heinlein themes and a repeated character and then to tie them together. The themes are liberty and libertarianism, and the unreality of the world. The character is the Heinlein Individual.

2. Liberty

From the very beginning of his writing career, liberty has been a favorite Heinlein subject. *"If This Goes On—,"* his first novel, is about a revolution fought against an authoritarian government. His second novel, *Sixth Column*, is about a revolution against an authoritarian invader. Heinlein has written at least five other novels about colonies winning their freedom and about wars fought to defend freedom against implacable invaders. The theme is a constant one.

Beyond this, however, Heinlein's stories are filled with strongly worded statements in favor of free-wheeling, far-reaching personal freedom:

> "It's neither your business, nor the business of this damn paternalistic government, to tell a man not to risk his life doing what he really wants to do." ("Requiem.")

> "The private life and free action of every individual must be scrupulously respected." (*Beyond This Horizon.*)

> The price of freedom is the willingness to do sudden battle, anywhere, any time and with utter recklessness. (*The Puppet Masters.*)

Most Heinlein stories yield similar statements—in his early stories in the statements of his characters, in his recent fiction in blunt, like-it-or-lump-it editorial opinion, as well. As can be seen from the quotations given above, Heinlein's idea of liberty is wolfish and thoroughgoing. To a certain extent Heinlein has always been at war with himself as to which aspect of his libertarianism would predominate. Liberty for the sharp-toothed or liberty for all? One example, particularly interesting for the manner in which Heinlein has reversed himself, can be found in *"If This Goes On—."*

In the original version of the story, the narrator writes:

> If we could capture New Jerusalem, there would then be time and opportunity to change the psychological conditioning of the people and make them aware that they really had been saved from a tyranny which had ruled by keeping them in ignorance, their minds chained.
>
> The plan concocted by Colonel Novak and Zebadiah provided for readjusting the people to freedom of thought and freedom of action. They planned nothing less than mass reorientation under hypnosis. The technique was simple, as simple as works of genius usually are. They had prepared a film which was a mixture of history, theological criticism, simple course in general science, exposition of the philosophy of the scientific viewpoint and frame of mind, and so forth. Taken consciously, it was too much to soak up in one dose, but they planned to use it on subjects in a state of light hypnosis.

Here, of course, the wolfishness predominates—like Deacon Mushrat of *Pogo*, who means to have peace even if he has to ram it down people's bloodthirsty throats, Heinlein's people are going to dispense liberty even if they have to brainwash people into accepting it.

In the revised and expanded version of the story, however, Heinlein brings all his heavy guns to bear on his former position and destroys it completely. The movie is still present in the story in an even more convincing and overwhelming form, but this time around Novak and Zeb Jones, both sympathetic characters, are not responsible for it. In this version, it was put together by an unsympathetic, eager-beaver underling against Novak's recommendation. Heinlein intensifies the original situation by having the eager-beaver say happily:

> ". . . this film, used with the preparatory technique and possibly in some cases with a light dose of one of the hypnotic drugs, can be depended on to produce an optimum political temperament in 83% of the populace."

But Heinlein then destroys the position. An elderly man whom the narrator likens in appearance to Mark Twain stands up and begins to speak:

> "I have a brother, as good a man as I am, but we haven't spoken in many years—because he is honestly devout in the established faith and he suspects me of heresy. Now this cub, with his bulging forehead and his whirling lights, would 'condition' my brother to make him 'politically reliable.' " . . .
> "Free men aren't 'conditioned!' Free men are free because they are ornery and cussed and prefer to arrive at their own prejudices in their own way—not have them spoonfed by a self-appointed mind tinkerer! We haven't fought, our brethren haven't bled and died, just to change bosses, no matter how sweet their motives."

And then to add punctuation, Heinlein has this old man drop dead just before the vote is taken on whether or not to use the film. The vote, of course, is not to use it.

Heinlein not only has a taste for free men, but for free societies as well. In *Beyond This Horizon* and in "Coventry" he presents two specifically libertarian societies, the sort of contexts in which every man can operate as freely as one can imagine under any government. Neither is perfect, or even perfectly imagined—not surprising when you consider the complexity and internal contradictions present in modern society—but both are very interesting.

There is a strong element of wolfishness present again in *Beyond This Horizon*. The social insurance of mutual respect of rights is the necessity to defend one's conduct with a gun. Theoretically, this means that the ordinary person will be polite and mind his own business lest he be challenged for his behavior. The flaw, of course, is that the man with a fast finger on the trigger would be forgiven conduct that another man would be held to account for. On the other hand, I'm not completely sure that Heinlein would regard this as a flaw.

In the world of "Coventry," social insurance is the Covenant. The judge who sentences the protagonist to Coventry gives a full account of what the Covenant is:

> "The Covenant is not a superstition, but a simple temporal contract entered into by those same revolutionists for pragmatic reasons. They wished to insure the maximum possible liberty for every person.
>
> "You yourself have enjoyed that liberty. No possible act, nor mode of conduct, was forbidden to you, as long as your action did not damage another. . . .
>
> "You complain that our way of living is dull and unromantic, and imply that we have deprived you of excitement to which you feel entitled. You are free to hold and express your esthetic opinion of our way of living, but you must not expect us to live to suit your tastes. You are free to seek danger and adventure if you wish— there is danger still in experimental laboratories; there is hardship in the mountains of the Moon, and death in the jungles of Venus— but you are not free to expose us to the violence of your nature."

Granted that we have a very exact idea of what constitutes damaging another person—and the ultimate definition might include simple breathing—this seems at least a fair statement of the aims of a libertarian society.

It seems to me that there are three ways in which a character with freedom of action can operate. He can operate within the framework of society, whether or not he is in full accord with it. He can reject society and strike out on his own. Or he can arbitrarily run society to suit himself. Heinlein has written of characters who do each of these things.

The hero of *Beyond This Horizon* is a perfect example of the first mode. He is a strong man, dissatisfied with both himself and his society, but when it is suggested to him that he join a revolution and change things to suit himself, he doesn't even consider the idea for a moment. He is too much a part of his society to reject it. Instead he achieves his aims by getting the society to agree to try things his way. The hero of *Double Star*, who becomes a professional politician, is another example, and so even is Harriman (the man who finances the first two trips to the Moon) who, though he may come within a hairsbreadth of illegality, always plays by the rules of society. In the same way, the hero of *Tunnel in the Sky* helps to found a society and then is treated shabbily by it, but nonetheless resists the suggestion of leaving the society and striking out on his own.

Heinlein has written three times of the man who finds his freedom in rejecting society, in "Waldo," in "Coventry" and in *Farnham's Freehold*. In the first two cases Heinlein's point is that the central characters are wrong in rejecting society.

Waldo, if you will recall, is a genius affected by a degenerative muscle disease who lives in a satellite home popularly known as "Wheelchair." That isn't Waldo's own name for it. He calls it "Freehold," and fondly thinks that while he is there he is not involved in what happens on Earth: " 'I have no interest in such troubles; I'm independent of such things.' " His mentor goes to considerable length to point out to him that he is not independent, that "Freehold" would not exist at all without society and society's technology. And Waldo ultimately forsakes his "independence" in order to take a place in normal society.

The point of "Coventry," too, is that the rugged individualist is not quite so much his own man as he believes that he is. Heinlein points this out directly. He says:

> The steel tortoise gave MacKinnon a feeling of Crusoe-like independence. It did not occur to him his chattel was the end product of the cumulative effort and intelligent co-operation of hundreds of thousands of men, living and dead.

And Heinlein spends more than a page elaborating this moral.

Perhaps one measure of the change in Heinlein in recent years is that *Farnham's Freehold* seriously sets forth the point of view that "Waldo" and "Coventry" reject. Hugh Farnham, as far as we can see, does not and will not function within modern society; the reaction of this competent man is to dig a competent hole in the ground to hide in. And then just as Waldo had his "Freehold," Farnham has his, kept independent of the rest of the world by mines, wire, and rifle bullets. It is an odd sort of freedom.

The third category is illustrated by two stories, "Lost Legacy" and "Gulf," in which Heinlein's characters make decisions for society by themselves and then enforce their decisions. In "Lost Legacy," the "enemy" are:

> . . . the antagonists of human liberty, of human dignity — the racketeers, the crooked political figures, the shysters, the dealers in phony religions, the sweat-shoppers, the petty authoritarians, all of the key figures among the traffickers in human misery and human oppression, themselves somewhat adept in the arts of the mind, and acutely aware of the danger of free knowledge—all of this unholy breed.

The good guys save society by deciding who the bad guys are and disposing of them.

In "Gulf," the sides are just as clearly drawn.

> "Some one must be on guard if the race is to live; there is no one but us. To guard effectively we New Men must be organized, must never fumble any crisis like this—and must increase our numbers. We are few now, Joe; as the crises increase, we must increase to meet them. Eventually—and it's a dead race with time—we must take over and make certain that baby never plays with matches. . . .
>
> "I confess to that same affection for democracy, Joe. But it's like yearning for the Santa Claus you believed in as a child. For a hundred and fifty years or so democracy, or something like it, could flourish safely. The issues were such as to be settled without disaster by the votes of common men, befogged and ignorant as they were. But now, if the race is simply to stay alive, political decisions depend on real knowledge of such things as nuclear physics, planetary ecology, genetic theory, even system mechanics. They aren't up to it, Joe. With goodness and more will than they possess less than one in a thousand could stay awake over one page of nuclear physics; they can't learn what they must know."

The answer is clear as to what course the "New Men" must take:

> "Joe, didn't you ever feel a yen to wipe out some evil, obscene,

> rotten jerk who infected everything he touched, yet was immune to legal action? We treat them as cancers; we excise them from the body social. We keep a 'Better Dead' list; when a man is clearly morally bankrupt we close his account at the first opportunity."

This again is a wolfish sort of freedom.

It is passages such as these from "Lost Legacy" and "Gulf" that caused me to think for a time that Heinlein was an authoritarian, but he is not. His characters ask no one to follow and obey them except from choice. Even the subordinates in Heinlein's military stories are always volunteers.

The judge in "Coventry" says to David MacKinnon:

> ". . . but your psychometrical tests show that you believe yourself capable of judging morally your fellow citizens and feel justified in personally correcting and punishing their lapses. . . . From a social standpoint, your delusion makes you mad as the March Hare."

If you allow the possibility of doubt as to their inborn *rightness*, the characters of "Gulf" and "Lost Legacy" are not sane. But they are not authoritarians.

Heinlein's characters are not democrats, either, as witness the quotation above from "Gulf," or the following passage from *Glory Road*:

> "Democracy can't work. Mathematicians, peasants, and animals, that's all there is—so democracy, a theory based on the assumption that mathematicians and peasants are equal, can never work. Wisdom is not additive; its maximum is that of the wisest man in a given group."

Since Heinlein writes about the wisest and most competent men that he can imagine, he doesn't even expect them to be democrats and I can't think of any who are. *Double Star*, for instance, the most democratic of Heinlein's stories, ends on a paternalistic, God-bless-the-little-people note:

> But there is solemn satisfaction in doing the best you can for eight billion people. Perhaps their lives have no cosmic significance, but they have feelings. They can hurt.

What Heinlein is, of course, is an elitist. Not only are his central characters Heinlein Individuals, and hence special, but Heinlein most often assigns his lead characters uncommon talents that set them even further apart. The hero of *The Puppet Masters* has a camera eye; the hero of *Citizen of the Galaxy* has an eidetic memory; the hero of *Glory Road* can unfailingly orient himself; the heroes of "Misfit" and *Starman Jones* are lightning calculators; the hero of *Time for the Stars* is a telepath; the hero of *Stranger in a Strange Land* can do almost anything with mind alone. Heinlein's elite is one of competence rather than of money or blood, and these special talents, by increasing competence, are added reason for the existence of the elite. In "Lost Legacy," these super powers are the single characteristic of the elite.

And of course, when the case for the right of the elite to rule is made, it is generally, as in "Gulf," made on the basis of competence. Competence proves itself.

Heinlein carries his elitism beyond individual characters to Man as an animal. He has a set piece—Man is "the most ravenous, intolerant, deadly, and successful of the animals in the explored universe"—that he has presented as a given at least five times: in *The Puppet Masters*, *Tunnel in the Sky*, *Starman Jones*, *Starship Troopers*, and in his prophecy article in the April 1956 *Amazing* where it is stated as an idea that will eventually be generally accepted.

In *Starship Troopers* the notion is editorially presented as a problem in morality. Does Man have the right to breed his way across the universe, filling it to the brim? The answer is that we will find out. If we get slapped down, then we didn't have the right. In other words, what can be gotten away with is "right." Following the same thought, the female lead in *Glory Road* is head of the Twenty Universes just as long as her competence keeps her alive; until then her decisions are *right*. They are automatically carried out because she is acknowledged to be more competent than everybody else. Someday she will be assassinated and then, because she is dead, she will be wrong, just as Man will be wrong if some other race knocks him off. This elitism, then, is the source of Heinlein's wolfishness. The fast-gun morality of *Beyond This Horizon* is acceptable—no, desirable—because it allows competence the chance to demonstrate itself.

Being four-square for liberty is a very easy and comfortable thing in the abstract. But in practice, there arise two other questions: "Liberty for whom?" and "Liberty to do what?" Heinlein's stories are varied enough so that neither question can be given a final answer that does not allow an exception to be produced. However, it is my feeling that the importance of liberty to Heinlein comes in relation to his competent men; they require freedom to become fully themselves. Freedom for the man who cannot stay awake over a page of nuclear physics is less important than for the man with the quick mind and the quick gun simply because the first man is less capable of doing anything with freedom were he to have it. In other words, freedom is the Heinlein Individual's right to do as he pleases, to make of himself what he can.

3. The Heinlein Individual

To an extent, the chief characters of any writer are likely to resemble their creator. As the character is the child of his creator, he resembles him. As a writer assigns his own opinions, attitudes and interests to a sympathetic character, so the character is likely to sound like him. This does not happen in the case of every man who writes, but it isn't uncommon in the case of a writer like Heinlein who has a distinct point of view to sell, and it is to this extent that I believe the Heinlein Individual resembles Heinlein himself.

The Heinlein Individual has three central characteristics: his strength, his singularity, and his ability to teach himself.

All three stages of the Heinlein Individual are strong and competent. The youngest stage may be ignorant and naive but that is an accident of youth and not a character deficiency. Young Andrew Jackson Libby, the protagonist of Heinlein's second story, "Misfit," is an example: he is innocent and ignorant, but at the same time he is bright, has a special talent (lightning calculation), and is both eager to learn and eager to please.

The naiveté of the first-stage Heinlein Individual leads him into error from which he is commonly extracted by his competence after he learns what he has to know. This makes him ripe for a "Man-Who-Learned-Better" situation. John Lyle, who learns that the Prophet is not above question in *"If This Goes On—,"* is one example and so is Don Harvey, the young hero of *Between Planets* who learns that there are times when political neutrality is not possible.

Since the first-stage Heinlein Individual is so often a sheep ripe for shearing, Heinlein has almost always provided him with a mentor in the form of an older Heinlein Individual. Michael Smith of *Stranger in a Strange Land* might well serve as an example of the supreme innocent—he has been brought up by Martians and knows nothing about human ways—and he has Jubal Harshaw, a man who is a doctor, a lawyer, and a popular writer, in short a man who knows all the essential things about human ways, to serve as his tutor. In the same way, Don Harvey falls under the wing of cynical old Dr. Jefferson, a Thorby has his Colonel Baslim, and John Lyle has Zeb Jones.

Zeb Jones, "the wiseacre without whom no Heinlein story is complete," to quote Damon Knight,* is an archetypical second-stage Heinlein Individual, the competent man in full bloom. This stage is less eager, more cynical, more likely to make a wisecrack than to rush out to save the world. The cynicism, no doubt, is the result of the destroyed past illusions of a former first-stage Heinlein Individual. Jones himself is a master psychologist, master fencer, master of palace politics; he knows everything that his protégé, Lyle, needs to learn.

In the same way, in *Starman Jones*, young Jones is taken in hand by Sam Anderson who wipes his nose, gets Jones' appearance changed, procures false papers for them both, tutors Jones and sneaks him aboard a starship. And Anderson knows his way around a starship well enough to keep Jones from suffering for his ignorance. Anderson even dies while rescuing Jones from trouble he has fallen into.

Perhaps the best description of the abilities of the second-stage Heinlein Individual comes from *Beyond This Horizon*:

> "I could set you down on an island peopled by howling savages and dangerous animals—in two weeks you would own the place. . . . You've got the physique and the mentality and the temperament."

* *In Search of Wonder*, 2nd ed., p. 77

The third-stage Heinlein Individual, perhaps because he has lost his energy, perhaps simply because he has lived longer, is even more cynical:

> "My dear, I used to think I was serving humanity . . . and I pleasured in the thought. Then I discovered that humanity does not want to be served; on the contrary it resents any attempt to serve it. So now I do what pleases Jubal Harshaw."

The major difference, however, between a Zeb Jones and a Colonel Dubois is that a Jones knows *how* things work, while a Dubois knows *why*, as well. This makes him an even more effective mentor, and this is the role a third-stage Heinlein Individual most often takes. Jubal Harshaw, the mentor of Michael Smith, the human Martian, is the one human who knows enough to explain things to Smith and, moreover, is the one human who knows enough to "grok the fullness" without knowing Martian.

This third stage serves as mentor not only to his young innocent counterpart but to his knowledgeable second-stage self as well. For instance, the head of the super-secret intelligence organization in *The Puppet Masters* is both father and mentor to the book's narrator, who is his chief agent. In "Waldo," Waldo is given advice by old Dr. Grimes, the one person he will listen to.

This continuing mentorship even forms a chain in several books, third stage lecturing second stage, and then second stage passing on advice to first stage, like a little girl solemnly telling her dolly to look both ways before crossing. *Beyond This Horizon* is one example. The third stage is Mordan Claude, District Moderator for Genetics and wise old man, who regularly counsels the novel's chief character, Hamilton Felix. Hamilton (the man with the physique, mentality and temperament to rule that wild island) in turn serves as advisor to his friend, Monroe-Alpha Clifford, who is an innocent for all his competence as an economist, and needs to be kept out of trouble.

There are, of course, clear intermediate examples of Heinlein Individuals. The narrator of *Farmer in the Sky* is not naive enough to be called a pure stage one, and his friend and sometime-mentor, Hank Jones, is not quite knowing or cynical enough to be a pure stage two. Roger Stone of *The Rolling Stones* and Hugh Farnham of *Farnham's*

Freehold seem to fall somewhere between stage two and stage three.

More than this, however, in two Heinlein stories we are given a view of a single character at all three stages—and serving as mentor to himself in full view, besides. The stories are "By His Bootstraps" and " 'All You Zombies—,' " both time travel stories.

In "By His Bootstraps," the hero, Bob Wilson, finds himself counseled by successive older selves, from slightly-more-knowledgeable to wise-old-man-who-knows-both-how-and-why. Then he himself inevitably acts out the roles he has already witnessed.

" 'All You Zombies—' " is more sophisticated and, in fact, very neatly symbolizes all the points we have considered. The first-stage ego of the story is a young girl, competent and ambitious, but innocent. The second stage (male) knows how the world wags but not why. He passes through time to meet his former female self and initiates her sexually, thereby ending her innocence. (And a more explicit sort of mentorship I can't imagine.) The third-stage ego, much older, knows why things have happened as they have. In his role as mentor he makes what has come before possible, including the ending of the innocence of his first self by his second and his own birth.

If there is one wish that all men have had at one time or another, it is that they might be able to go back and avoid the mistakes they once made and so save themselves a lot of pain. Heinlein has the perfect way to do this: his Individual, no matter the number of different guises he appears in, is one single character who quite conveniently serves as teacher to himself. In this way the man who has learned better can alert his naive self and save him the cost of his mistakes. The world may have to be tied into knots to allow the Heinlein Individual to prevail, but that is quite all right since he is the single, solitary real thing in an essentially unreal world. The world exists for him, not he for the world.

4. Unreality

Sheer continued existence seems to be something that is tremendously important to Heinlein, and a guarantee of it a necessary reassurance. His character Hamilton Felix in *Beyond This Horizon*, for instance, takes the promise of life after death in the form of re-incarnation as the *only* thing that gives life any point. The form of continued existence does vary, however, from one story to the next.

The easiest way is for his characters simply not to die. Suspended animation takes care of this in several of his stories—in *Tunnel in the Sky* suspended animation is used to keep a dying man alive long enough for techniques to save him to be developed, and this same suspended animation is brought into several other stories. *Methuselah's Children* is about nothing else than length of life: extension of it first by breeding for longevity and then by purely medical means. A psychological need for the postponement of death seems to grip the characters in the story to the point of monomania, as though the calm acceptance of death were not possible. One character, in fact, having lived about two hundred years and feeling death impending, chooses to give up her individuality and become part of a group mind simply to be able to avoid extinction.

In "Elsewhen," a Heinlein character says (supplying his own italics),

> "When you die, you won't die all over, no matter how intensely you may claim to expect to. *It is an emotional impossibility for any man to believe in his own death.*"

So, admitting the possibility of death of a sort, Heinlein has miti-gated it in several ways. Ghosts are one way—they linger on and in lingering deny the finality of death. The only flaw is that the power of the ghost to influence things through his continued existence is severely limited, so when Heinlein has introduced ghosts, they have been Martian ghosts (in *Red Planet* and *Stranger in a Strange Land*) rather than human ones.

Another way Heinlein has found of mitigating death is reincarna-tion, which, of course, does allow for effective action beyond death and so is suitable for Heinlein Individuals. Heinlein makes reincarna-tion an important minor thread of *Beyond This Horizon*, but his use of it in *Stranger in a Strange Land* is more revealing: in that story Martians become ghosts but human worthies are reincarnated.

As important as this denial of the reality of death is, however, just as important is a denial of the reality of the world, the only thing that can make the first denial meaningful. It is by his singular ability to transcend the bounds of the world that the Heinlein Individual demonstrates his difference from other humans. For instance, Waldo, in the story named after him, is able to make the world what he wants it to be by simply thinking it so and forcing his idea on everyone else. Similarly, in "Elsewhen" it is possible for the story protagonists to leave this world and travel to any number of other aspects of reality by thinking proper thoughts. It is by success that the Heinlein Individual reveals himself, including success in Heinlein's brand of transcendentalism.

With this in mind, it is interesting to look at one of the few quotations from Shakespeare that Heinlein has used in his stories. The quotation is particularly interesting since Heinlein has introduced it no less than four times—in *Between Planets*, *Double Star*, *Have Space Suit—Will Travel*, and *Farnham's Freehold*. The speech is from *The Tempest* and in full goes:

> Our revels now are ended. These our actors,
> As I foretold you, were all spirits, and
> Are melted into air, into thin air:
> And, like the baseless fabric of this vision,
> The cloud-capp'd towers, the gorgeous palaces,
> The solemn temples, the great globe itself,
> Yea, all which it inherit, shall dissolve,
> And, like this insubstantial pageant faded,
> Leave not a rack behind. We are such stuff
> As dreams are made on; and our little life
> Is rounded with a sleep.

This, of course, is a flat denial of the reality of the world. It is interesting, moreover, that for all that Heinlein has quoted from the passage, he has not quoted the last sentence. In other words, he is quite willing to chalk off the world but people are not quite so easily disposed of. In fact, at the time of the quotation's use in *Have Space Suit—Will Travel*, there is a threat that our world will be destroyed: the story protagonist—who has just done the quoting—says, apparently against all logic:

> "All right, take away our star— You will if you can and I guess you can. Go ahead! We'll *make* a star! Then, someday, we'll come back and hunt you down—*all of you!*"

In other words, the world may end, but wolfish men will survive.

The ultimately "real" Heinlein Individual, however, is the solipsist. A solipsist is a person who starts as Descartes did, with "I think, therefore I am," and then is unable to go further. He knows that *he* is, that he exists, but is not sure that the rest of us think and so is forced to doubt our reality; the world then becomes the conscious or unconscious product of the solipsist himself, the only real thing that exists. Heinlein played with the notion in *Beyond This Horizon* (which, remember, also deals with reincarnation). In this story it is suggested that the world is a game and all the characters of the story pieces in the game, some of them automatic and some not:

> You locked up your memory, and promised not to look, then played through the part you had picked with just the rules assigned to that player.

Solipsism forms the core of the short stories "They" and " 'All You Zombies—.' " In these stories the central point is not just that the main characters are solipsists—not so strange since many solipsists have lived and died since the world began—but that their solipsism is justified. They are, *in fact*, the points around which all the universe revolves.

A quotation from the central character of "They" may serve to sum up the essence of all Heinlein Individuals who outlive their worlds:

> "Second only to the prime datum of my own existence [*I think, therefore I am*] is the emotionally convincing certainty of my own continuity. I may be a closed curve, but, closed or open, I neither have a beginning nor an end. Self-awareness is not relational; it is absolute, and cannot be reached to be destroyed, or created."

It does not matter too much how, but the Heinlein Individual always goes on existing.

5. Import

To draw the threads together, then, the Heinlein Individual can be seen as the one real thing in an unreal world, quite naturally seeking to do as he pleases. You might even say that it is by doing as he pleases that he demonstrates his reality. Without his liberty, the Heinlein Individual becomes indistinguishable from the other shades and shadows that inhabit the worlds he plays his games in; with it he rules his worlds and survives their passing. And this is an indication of the basis as well as the limits of both Heinlein's elitism and his libertarianism.

Stranger in a Strange Land neatly demonstrates every one of the points that I have made. All men in this story are not equal. Some are real and some are not. The unreal ones are children of this world and perish with it; the real ones live after and added together form the only God there is. The theme of the book is, "All which groks is God," grokking being the ultimate understanding of why things are as they are, and Jubal Harshaw, the wise-old-man Heinlein Individual, being the ultimate example of one who groks. If you extrapolate this set to cover all of Heinlein's fiction and understand that the Heinlein Individual, no matter what story he is in, always groks, then the point should be clear.

" *'It is an emotional impossibility'* "—Heinlein says—" *'for any man to believe in his own death.'* " I doubt very strongly that this is true, but I suspect that it is true of Heinlein himself, who has, at the least, much in common with his Heinlein Individual. I suspect, too, that on an emotional level, Heinlein may be sure of his own abilities and suspicious of the abilities of the ordinary man. To this extent, I would call him an emotional solipsist. Intellectually he may still question, but his emotional inclinations, as demonstrated in story after story, are set.

In view of this, *Farnham's Freehold* takes on added interest. In this story, for all that the Heinlein Individual retains his competence he does not succeed. He is frustrated at every turn. Far from transcending the universe, he is subject to its whims, being flicked willy-nilly through time and from situation to situation, through all of which he remains essentially powerless. The Individual, Hugh Farnham, speaks continually of freedom and liberty, which, as usual, can be taken to mean the opportunity to do as he pleases. And the story as a whole can be taken as the search on Farnham's part for the simple situation that other Heinlein Individuals have had as a matter of course—a universe in which to be God. That universe, when he does find it and surrounds it with mines and barbed wire to keep it inviolate, is such a constricted pea patch as to be almost a symbol of failure. The story itself may symbolize the failure of Heinlein's long-held belief in the ability of the competent man to prevail eternally. If that belief has truly been lost, I cannot say for certain what will follow: perhaps the end of the Heinlein Individual. The essentially impotent spectator-narrator of *The Moon Is a Harsh Mistress* may perhaps be a sign of this.

VIII. HEINLEIN'S NON-FICTION

Since the main interest of this book is Robert Heinlein's science fiction, I've made no attempt to discuss his articles, lectures and speeches. However, it is quite true that a number of them are very interesting and have a certain pertinence to his science fiction, and hence deserve some discussion, if only briefly.

In recent years, science fiction has been a staple item with the large professional publishing houses, but twenty years ago this was not so. Science fiction was published by minor houses dedicated to digging out favorite stories from old magazines and putting them into hardcovers. In 1947, one of these houses, Fantasy Press, asked seven of its authors to contribute short articles to a symposium on science fiction writing. The book, *Of Worlds Beyond*, was out of print for years and so scarce that its editor could not even locate an extra copy, until it was recently reprinted by Advent:Publishers.

Robert Heinlein was one of the contributors to *Of Worlds Beyond*. His article was entitled "On the Writing of Speculative Fiction."

Although the title implies a general discussion, Heinlein quickly dismisses the gadget story and limits himself to stories about people. He says that there are three kinds: boy-meets-girl, The Little Tailor, and the-man-who-learned-better. He then discusses each of these. The first and last classes are self-explanatory; The Little Tailor is the story of the man who succeeds or fails spectacularly.

The main trouble with these classes, from my point of view, is that they are not exclusive. It isn't at all difficult to imagine a man learning the error of his ways, winning a girl, and succeeding wildly, all in one story. It also seems unlikely that a story would ever be conceived of in terms of these categories; they strike me as descriptive rather than prescriptive.

Heinlein then lists the conditions necessary for the making of a science fiction story: a respect for facts, a difference from the here-and-now essential to the story, and a human problem arising from the difference or affected by it. And by and large, this seems a good prescriptive list.

Heinlein concludes his article by discussing professional work habits and saying that these have more to do with successful speculative fiction than anything he had said before. This, too, strikes me as sound thinking, since there is nothing quite so fruitless as an unwritten story.

In 1957, lectures were delivered by Heinlein, C. M. Kornbluth, Robert Bloch, and Alfred Bester at the University of Chicago on the role of science fiction as social criticism, and in 1959, Advent:Publishers collected and published these lectures in a volume entitled *The Science Fiction Novel*, with a well-informed introduction by Basil Davenport. Heinlein's paper is entitled "Science Fiction: Its Nature, Faults and Virtues."

He begins by discussing the inadequacies of most definitions of science fiction, and accepting one by Reginald Bretnor,* which he summarizes:

> [Science fiction is that sort of literature] in which the author shows awareness of the nature and importance of the human activity known as the scientific method, shows equal awareness of the great body of human knowledge already collected through that activity, and takes into account in his stories the effects and possible future effects on human beings of scientific method and scientific fact.

I don't care for this definition myself—I much prefer the prescriptive list Heinlein himself set forth in *Of Worlds Beyond*. It seems

* *Modern Science Fiction*, p. 273.

to me that Bretnor's definition would let in not only *Arrowsmith*, as Davenport points out in his introduction, but Dr. Kildare, as well, and almost any novel about a laboratory or the new rash of stories written by people who have made a quick trip to Cape Kennedy.

Heinlein then separates fantasy and science fiction. Fantasy stories, to Heinlein, are imaginary-but-not-possible, while science fiction is realistic and about the possible. Science fiction can go contrary to theory, but not to fact—which to me makes *Stranger in a Strange Land* clearly not science fiction—while fantasy is always contrary to fact.

Heinlein then proposes another short definition of science fiction:

> Realistic speculation about possible future events, based solidly on adequate knowledge of the real world, past and present, and on a thorough understanding of the nature and significance of the scientific method.

Heinlein says this is a definition of almost all science fiction, and to make it complete we simply need strike out the word "future."

While this definition strikes me somewhat more favorably than Bretnor's does, it seems to me that Heinlein's qualification puts us back in the lab with Dr. Kildare again, and without the qualification, the definition eliminates stories like Poul Anderson's *The High Crusade*, Piper's Paratime stories, and all of the many stories that have aliens among us disguised as mail boxes.

Heinlein then goes on to discuss at length science fiction as it is. Except by accident it is not prophecy, and Heinlein gives examples from his own work to demonstrate this. He says that most of it is not very good as literature, partly because it is the most difficult sort of prose to write, and that much of it is not even entertaining—all points that seem to have a large measure of truth to them.

On the other hand, Heinlein finds science fiction the most alive, most important, most useful and most comprehensive fiction being written today. He finds its importance in its attempt to deal with the future, that being the only point of time we can affect at all. The difficulty in writing science fiction is in the body of knowledge it requires and the amount of directed imagination it takes, but since it does deal with change, the most important fact of our world, it is the only form of fiction that has any chance of interpreting our world. He concludes by saying that science fiction will never be mass entertainment, but that it should increase in amount and quality.

I don't fully agree with all these points, but I won't quarrel with them. My summary, no doubt, is unfairly compact, Heinlein's arguments are interesting and they do explain why he should spend his entire career writing almost nothing but science fiction. Feeling as he does, he could hardly do otherwise.

In the November 1952 *School Library Association of California Bulletin*, Robert Heinlein had an article entitled "Ray Guns and Rocket Ships," the general aim of which is to explain science fiction to the unbelievers. The first section is a historical summary. In the second section, Heinlein argues for calling the field "speculative fiction," which, he says, "may be defined negatively as being fiction about things that have not happened." In my opinion, Heinlein takes too big a mouthful here, since almost all fiction can be defined as being about things that have not happened. Heinlein goes on to make a case for the necessity of a wide field of knowledge for the writing and for the judging of science fiction. Finally, Heinlein speaks of children and science fiction. He says that science fiction for children ought to be of interest to adults, too, since "a book so juvenile that it will insult the intelligence of adults is quite likely to insult the intelligence of the kids," a refreshing stand to take. He says that his children's sf is marked from his adult fiction in two ways: "I place a little less emphasis on boy-meets-girl and a little more emphasis on unadulterated science."

The article is also noteworthy for the following preview of later things:

> You would not expect a Martian to be named Smith. (Say— how about a story about a Martian named 'Smith?' Ought to make a good short. Hmmm—)

On two separate occasions—in the February 1952 issue of *Galaxy*, and in the April 1956 issue of *Amazing*—Robert Heinlein has published articles attempting to predict something of the world of

2000 A.D. The *Amazing* article was quite short, the article in *Galaxy* more detailed.

The *Galaxy* article begins with contrasting looks at the world of 1900 and the world of 2000. Heinlein then says that his predictions—various gadgets, household nudity, etc.—are really quite timid, and that in actual fact we can expect changes in the next fifty years that are at least eight times as great as the changes of the past fifty years.

In light of this contention, Heinlein makes nineteen predictions, none of them particularly timid, justifying his lack of caution by saying that while some of these predictions will be wrong, timid predictions are certain to be wrong. His predictions include a solution to the housing problem through revolutionary technology by 1967, the disappearance of Communism, controlled gravity, and the discovery of intelligent life on Mars.

He continues with a list of things we *won't* have: travel faster than light, laboratory creation of life, a permanent end to war, and scientific proof of survival after death. (This last, in particular, seems to reflect one of Heinlein's personal concerns.)

Heinlein concludes with a brief discussion of new areas of concern in science, and science's greatest crisis: keeping tabs on the information we do have so that it can be *used*.

In 1966, in the collection *The Worlds of Robert A. Heinlein*, this article was reprinted under the title "Pandora's Box." The list of prophecies at the end of the original article was commented upon and brought up to date, and a new foreword to the article was included in which, among other things, Heinlein says, "the science fiction writer—*any* fiction writer—must keep entertainment consciously in mind as his prime purpose," a dictum I wish he had paid closer attention to in recent years.

The *Amazing* article is a retrospective look from the year 2000, listing advances. His predictions include the use of telepathy and clairvoyance for military purposes, acceptance of man's nature as a wild animal and the toughest creature in these parts (a favorite Heinlein notion), and—reversing the position taken in the earlier article—a certainty of survival after death.

In April of 1958, the Committee for a Sane Nuclear Policy ran an ad in a number of newspapers across the country calling on the President to end our testing of nuclear weapons. On Sunday, April 13, Robert Heinlein and his wife answered it in a full-page ad in the Colorado Springs *Gazette Telegraph* headlined:

Who Are The Heirs Of Patrick Henry?
Stand Up And Be Counted!

The ad is laced with the following quotations in boldface:

> Is life so dear, or peace so sweet, as to be purchased at the price of chains and slavery? Forbid it, Almighty God! I know not what course others may take, but as for me, *give me liberty, or give me death!!*

> The Mice Voted to Bell the Cat.

> "Will you walk into my parlor?" said the Spider to the Fly.

> God grants liberty only to those who love it and are always ready to guard and defend it.

> They that can give up essential liberty to obtain a little temporary safety deserve neither liberty nor safety.

> The liberties of our country, the freedom of our civil Constitution, are worth defending at all hazards.

Heinlein states that whether or not those signing the Sane Committee ad are Communists, the ad itself is the rankest sort of Communist propaganda, and he rejects its three proposals. Giving up nuclear weapons leaves 170 million of us to stand against 900 million of them. Other-than-on-the-spot-inspection leaves the Russians free to conduct secret and undetectable underground bomb tests. And putting missiles under United Nations control is likewise folly. To Heinlein, the Sane Committee proposals amount to outright surrender to the Communists: "Those who signed that manifesto have made their choice; consciously or unconsciously they prefer enslavement to death." He suggests that those who agree with him write to the President calling on Mr. Eisenhower to ignore the Sane Committee proposals—and he provides a letter for people to copy and sign if they wish. He also suggests the foundation of "The Patrick Henry League" to prove that the Spirit of '76 is not dead.

Heinlein's ad, it seems to me, is very definitely related to his fiction, particularly that from his third period. It reflects his concern with liberty, it couches moral matters in black-and-white terms, and it is clearly polemical. Its closest fictional relatives are probably *The Puppet Masters*, *Farnham's Freehold*, and *Starship Troopers*. *Starship Troopers*, in fact, was the first Heinlein novel to be written after Heinlein's ad and it seems an attempt to make many of the same arguments in fictional form.

On two occasions, Robert Heinlein has been Guest of Honor at World Science Fiction Conventions—at the Third Convention, held in Denver in 1941, and at the Nineteenth Convention, held in Seattle twenty years later. On both of these occasions Heinlein delivered speeches of interest, and the second quite deliberately examines some of the same territory as the first.

The 1941 speech was a rambling discussion entitled "The Discovery of the Future." The major portion of it is given up to the importance of being concerned with the future—not just a few days, but as great a period as can be imagined. Heinlein labels this "timebinding," a term he credits to Korzybski, and says this concern is the activity that most strongly separates humans from other animals.

Heinlein then makes predictions for the immediate years ahead: mass insanity and a series of wars lasting up to fifty years. The one thing that would serve as self-protection for the human race would be the use of the scientific method—the only basis for sanity being to distinguish facts and non-facts clearly.

This concern for facts above all else, of course, has been a distinguishing characteristic of Heinlein's fiction from the very first.

The 1961 speech was entitled "The Future Revisited," and was extremely rambling and apparently extemporaneous. It begins with a claim that the mass insanity and wars predicted twenty years earlier have actually transpired.

Heinlein then divides the possible futures he sees for us into two groups: an unlikely 10%—the sun going nova, Khrushchev becoming a Christian, peace in the world—and a likely 90%. In this 90%, there are exactly three possibilities: Russia destroys us in a war; we collapse internally and give up to Russia; or we and Russia destroy each other and China wins. In any case, no matter which of these possibilities comes to pass, one-third of us die.

Heinlein's attitude is that since we are going to lose in any case, we might as well go down fighting. We ought to stock bomb shelters—something Heinlein himself has done since—and acquire unregistered weapons, and then die as gloriously as possible.

The relation of these ideas to Heinlein's fiction—again particularly that of his third period—is obvious. Hugh Farnham of *Farnham's Freehold* is an example of a character who has followed Heinlein's advice to the letter.

At this point, Heinlein strikes off on a new tangent, listing three things that are of supreme importance to him—he says he would not jail anyone, enslave anyone (he includes the draft as a form of slavery), or suppress information. He states this as his mature opinion since, he says, in his adult lifetime he has commanded conscripts, sent people to jail, and stamped information secret.

Of the three things vital to him, Heinlein picks one—free circulation of information—as one of the reasons for his opposition to Communism, and tells of experiences traveling in Russia that convinced him that the Russians do toy with the truth. Many of the same anecdotes, by the way, are recounted in an article by Heinlein in the October 1960 issue of the *American Mercury*, an article worth reading, if for no other reason, for the report of a quizzing in a Kazakstan commissar's office in which Heinlein got thoroughly mad and Mrs. Heinlein started pointing out the location of slave labor camps on the map.

The major difference between the two speeches as I read one and heard the other is a hardening on Heinlein's part that seems reflected in his fiction. The 1941 Heinlein is a more tentative, less dogmatic, and more approachable man than the self he shows in his later speech. The change, I think, has hurt his fiction, and is to be regretted.

Bibliography—Heinlein's Non-Fiction

1941

The Discovery of the Future — Guest of Honor speech, Third World Science Fiction Convention, Denver

1947

Back of the Moon — Article, *Elks Magazine*, January 1947

Flight into the Future — Article, *Collier's*, August 30, 1947 (with Caleb B. Laning)

On the Writing of Speculative Fiction — Essay, OF WORLDS BEYOND

1950

Shooting "Destination Moon" — Article, *Astounding Science Fiction*, July 1950

Preface — THE MAN WHO SOLD THE MOON

1952

Where To? — Article, *Galaxy Science Fiction*, Feb. 1952

Introduction — TOMORROW, THE STARS

Ray Guns and Rocket Ships — Article, *School Library Association of California Bulletin*, Nov. 1952

1953

Concerning Stories Never Written — Preface, REVOLT IN 2100

Introduction — THE BEST FROM STARTLING STORIES

1956

As I See Tomorrow — Article, *Amazing Stories*, April 1956

1958

Who Are the Heirs of Patrick Henry? — Advertisement, *Colorado Springs Telegraph Gazette*, April 13, 1958

1959

Science Fiction: Its Nature, Faults and Virtues — Essay, THE SCIENCE FICTION NOVEL

1960

Pravda Means "Truth" — Article, *American Mercury*, October 1960

1961

The Future Revisited — Guest of Honor speech, Nineteenth World Science Fiction Convention, Seattle

1963

All Aboard the Gemini — Article, *Popular Mechanics*, May 1963

1966

Pandora's Box — Introduction, THE WORLDS OF ROBERT A. HEINLEIN

IX. THE FUTURE OF HEINLEIN

There is an amount of presumption in any critical book, and perhaps altogether too much in any critical book that deals with a particular author, especially one who is still living. The final presumption in such a case is a chapter of conclusions. On the one hand, the form of a book demands that having spent 70,000 words in sketching a writer's career and discussing his methods and his attitudes, a critic should put some sort of capstone in place. On the other, the writer may not be ready for any sort of capstone, let alone a monument and epitaph. It may well be that Heinlein has a Fourth, Fifth and Sixth Period ahead of him. He may even be in a new period right now that I am too near to discern clearly.

If I were to guess where Heinlein is going from here and were wrong, I would look foolish. If I were to guess where Heinlein is going from here and were right, I would sound either sycophantic or impertinent—and possibly both. I prefer to look on this book as an interim report, and one that can and should be argued with. Even in the ground that it covers, there remains much to be said. I hope others will take the time to say it.

Still, I think this book demands a conclusion. Rather than talk of Heinlein's immediate future, however, I'd like to leave his career still open-ended and talk instead of Heinlein's ultimate place in science fiction and his final stature as a writer, something remote enough to be relatively unembarrassing.

It is clear right now that even if his career were to be over, Heinlein would retain a historical place in company with Wells and Stapledon. Awards would be named after him, his name would be cited, and his health would be drunk. This historical position has two bases.

The first of these is the story-telling techniques that Heinlein developed and that have been generally copied within the field. It is these, I think, that caused de Camp's eighteen leading writers in 1953 to name Heinlein as the only contemporary science fiction writer who had influenced them. I can't help but believe that a similar poll taken today would again acknowledge Heinlein's influence.

Most of the stories of the thirties were not basically extrapolative. They depended on color, flash, movement, and raw idea, and they were comparatively lacking in detail and a concern for consequence. Heinlein showed that it was possible to have both detail and consequence without any loss of dramatic impact and with a very definite gain in verisimilitude.

The last twenty-five years of science fiction may even be taken in large part as an exploration by many writers of the possibilities inherent in Heinlein's techniques. It is this shift from basically speculative stories to basically extrapolative stories that accounts, I think, for Sam Moskowitz's lost sense of wonder. I think there are evidences now of a shift back toward speculation, but these new speculative stories differ from the old ones in being built on an extrapolative base. Heinlein's insistence in talking clearly, knowledgeably, and dramatically about the real world destroyed forever the sweet, pure, wonderful innocence that science fiction once had. However, it cost it none of its range of possibility, and in fact, even extended its range. It simply killed innocence. In a sense, Heinlein may be said to have offered science fiction a road to adulthood.

The second basis for Heinlein's importance in science fiction is his position as the first, and so far, the most serious exponent of a particular sort of story.

It is fair, I think, to say that there are four general types of science fiction stories, plus various hybrids. The four are adventure, satirical, extrapolative, and speculative. The techniques of extrapolation that Heinlein developed are equally applicable to all four.

Heinlein himself has most often applied his techniques to extrapolative stories. Other authors have done as much—*Mission of Gravity* is an extrapolative story that is totally unlike anything Heinlein has ever done—it is a particular type of extrapolative story that Heinlein can take credit for.

Most science fiction, even basically extrapolative science fiction, has concentrated almost as a matter of course on the atypical situation, the abnormal, the extraordinary. It has never been willing to stand still and examine the ordinary person functioning normally in a strange context. Yet life today and life yesterday have both been composed most commonly of the routines of living. There is no reason to suppose that tomorrow won't be the same.

The problem has been that science fiction has been a pulp literary form, and without any question by anyone has automatically served us pulp plots, pulp motivations, and pulp action-for-the-sake-of-action. We want variety in our fiction, to be sure, but *the future is already strange*. We don't *have* to compound the strangeness by tossing in monsters, revolts, chases, fights, torture, Imperial Guards, people-eating machines, and fertility rituals. There is room enough for drama without them. As Damon Knight has said, "Let us sit still, and unroll our mats, and tell our tales."* There is true drama and unlimited possibility in stories about people who live lives that are strange to us, but normal to them.

Robert Heinlein is the one science fiction writer who has regularly dealt with the strange-but-normal. Most often this has been in terms of chapters, or in short stories. Occasionally, as in *Farmer in the Sky*, it has been in whole books. He may not have taken this sort of story as far as it can go, but he has made possible those first-rate stories on this model that are yet to be written. If there is as much potential in this vein as I believe, it is added reason to honor Heinlein's name.

To be a historical figure, however, says nothing about literary currency. What sort of reputation is Heinlein likely to achieve? Which of his books are likely to continue to be read?

This depends in part on the future of science fiction. Heinlein is

_____
* *In Search of Wonder*, 2nd ed., p. 253.

bound so inextricably with science fiction that if the field were to fail, so would Heinlein.

Science fiction will probably never become much more widely popular than it is now, but I think it is likely to receive increasing amounts of serious critical attention and regard, and its unique possibilities and qualities are likely to be more widely recognized than they presently are. This should happen when science fiction loses its pulp odor—and that, I suspect, will occur when the science fiction magazines finally die. If science fiction does eventually attract serious consideration, then necessarily so will Heinlein. Heinlein is bound inextricably with science fiction, but the bonds are just as clear the other way: Heinlein is a dominating figure in science fiction.

I would not be surprised to see Heinlein's reputation come eventually to resemble that of Kipling. I am far from the first to notice their similarities. Their temperaments seem similar. Their attitudes toward life seem similar. I think their reputations may come to be similar, too, specifically in two regards. I think English letters will grant both small, secure places. I think that security will be increased by the fact that unlike many important writers of the past—including some of greater importance than either Kipling or Heinlein—both men will continue to be read, and by a similar audience. Today, Kipling is principally read by children—if any of his work is neglected, it is that which was written specifically for adults. *Kim*, *"Captains Courageous," The Jungle Books*, and *Puck of Pook's Hill* are the Kipling that continues to live. In the same way, if Heinlein becomes neglected, I think it is his work for adults that will suffer. I have no doubt that *Red Planet*, *Starman Jones*, and *Have Space Suit—Will Travel* will continue to hold readers for a good many years.

This assessment is merely a conjecture, of course—but I can't help thinking that Kipling would enjoy having Heinlein in his corner. They'd have things to talk about.

APPENDIX

1. Bibliography of Critical Works on the Field of Science Fiction

A few other such books have been published, but these are the ones that I have found to be of interest and of use.

Amis, Kingsley. NEW MAPS OF HELL. Harcourt, Brace and Co., New York, 1960.

Atheling, William, Jr. [James Blish]. THE ISSUE AT HAND. Advent:Publishers, Chicago, 1964.

Bretnor, Reginald, ed. MODERN SCIENCE FICTION. Coward-McCann, Inc., New York, 1953.

Davenport, Basil. INQUIRY INTO SCIENCE FICTION. Longmans, Green and Co., New York, 1955.

Davenport, Basil, and others. THE SCIENCE FICTION NOVEL. Advent:Publishers, Chicago, 1959.

De Camp, L. Sprague. SCIENCE-FICTION HANDBOOK. Hermitage House, New York, 1953.

Eshbach, Lloyd Arthur, ed. OF WORLDS BEYOND. Fantasy Press, Reading, Pa., 1947; Advent:Publishers, Chicago, 1964.

Knight, Damon. IN SEARCH OF WONDER. Advent:Publishers, Chicago, 1956; rev. ed., 1967.

Moskowitz, Sam. EXPLORERS OF THE INFINITE. World Publishing Co., Cleveland, 1963.

Moskowitz, Sam. SEEKERS OF TOMORROW. World Publishing Co., Cleveland, 1965.

Rogers, Alva. A REQUIEM FOR ASTOUNDING. Advent:Publishers, Chicago, 1964.

2. Chronological Bibliography of Science Fiction by Robert Heinlein

Included are the first publication of short stories, original paperback editions, and all hardcover titles published in the United States.

1939

Life-Line	*Astounding Science Fiction*, Aug. 1939
Misfit	*Astounding Science Fiction*, Nov. 1939

1940

Requiem	*Astounding Science Fiction*, Jan. 1940
"If This Goes On—"	*Astounding Science Fiction*, Feb., March 1940
"Let There Be Light"	*Super Science Stories*, May 1940 (by Lyle Monroe)
The Roads Must Roll	*Astounding Science Fiction*, June 1940
Coventry	*Astounding Science Fiction*, July 1940
Blowups Happen	*Astounding Science Fiction*, Sept. 1940
The Devil Makes the Law (Magic, Inc.)	*Unknown*, Sept. 1940

1941

Sixth Column	*Astounding Science Fiction*, Jan., Feb., March 1941 (by Anson MacDonald)
"And He Built a Crooked House"	*Astounding Science Fiction*, Feb. 1941
Logic of Empire	*Astounding Science Fiction*, March 1941
Beyond Doubt	*Astonishing Stories*, April 1941 (by Lyle Monroe and Elma Wentz
They	*Unknown*, April 1941
Solution Unsatisfactory	*Astounding Science Fiction*, May 1941 (by Anson MacDonald)
Universe	*Astounding Science Fiction*, May 1941
Methuselah's Children	*Astounding Science Fiction*, July, Aug., Sept. 1941
"—We Also Walk Dogs"	*Astounding Science Fiction*, July 1941 (by Anson MacDonald)
Elsewhere (Elsewhen)	*Astounding Science Fiction*, Sept. 1941 (by Caleb Saunders)
By His Bootstraps	*Astounding Science Fiction*, Oct. 1941 (by Anson MacDonald)
Common Sense	*Astounding Science Fiction*, Oct. 1941

Lost Legion   *Super Science Stories*, Nov. 1941 (by Lyle
   (Lost Legacy)   Monroe)

1942

"My Object All Sublime"   *Future*, Feb. 1942 (by Lyle Monroe)
Goldfish Bowl   *Astounding Science Fiction*, March 1942
                            (by Anson MacDonald)
Pied Piper   *Astonishing Stories*, March 1942 (by Lyle
                            Monroe)
Beyond This Horizon   *Astounding Science Fiction*, April, May
                            1942 (by Anson MacDonald)
Waldo   *Astounding Science Fiction*, Aug. 1942
                            (by Anson MacDonald)
The Unpleasant Profession of   *Unknown Worlds*, Oct. 1942 (by John
   Jonathan Hoag   Riverside)

1943–1946

no fiction published

1947

The Green Hills of Earth   *Saturday Evening Post*, Feb. 8, 1947
Space Jockey   *Saturday Evening Post*, April 26, 1947
Columbus Was a Dope   *Startling Stories*, May 1947 (by Lyle
                            Monroe)
It's Great to Be Back   *Saturday Evening Post*, July 26, 1947
Jerry Is a Man   *Thrilling Wonder Stories*, Oct. 1947
   (Jerry Was a Man)
Water Is for Washing   *Argosy*, Nov. 1947
ROCKET SHIP GALILEO   Scribner's (original juvenile novel)

1948

The Black Pits of Luna   *Saturday Evening Post*, Jan. 10, 1948
Gentlemen, Be Seated!   *Argosy*, May 1948
Ordeal in Space   *Town and Country*, May 1948
BEYOND THIS HORIZON   Fantasy Press (novel, serialized 1942)
SPACE CADET   Scribner's (original juvenile novel)

1949

Our Fair City   *Weird Tales*, Jan. 1949
Nothing Ever Happens on the Moon   *Boys' Life*, April, May 1949
Gulf   *Astounding Science Fiction*, Nov., Dec.
                            1949

Delilah and the Space-Rigger	*Blue Book*, Dec. 1949
The Long Watch	*American Legion Magazine*, Dec. 1949
RED PLANET	Scribner's (original juvenile novel)
SIXTH COLUMN	Gnome Press (novel, serialized 1941)

1950

Satellite Scout (Farmer in the Sky)	*Boys' Life*, Aug., Sept., Oct., Nov. 1950
Destination Moon	*Short Stories Magazine*, Sept. 1950
The Man Who Sold the Moon	(original story in book of the same title)
FARMER IN THE SKY	Scribner's (juvenile novel, serialized 1950)
THE MAN WHO SOLD THE MOON	Shasta (collection: Life-Line, 1939; "Let There Be Light," 1940; The Roads Must Roll, 1940; Blowups Happen, 1940; The Man Who Sold the Moon, 1950; Requiem, 1940)
WALDO AND MAGIC, INC.	Doubleday (two stories, 1940 and 1942)

1951

Planets in Combat (Between Planets)	*Blue Book*, Sept., Oct. 1951
The Puppet Masters	*Galaxy Science Fiction*, Sept., Oct., Nov. 1951
BETWEEN PLANETS	Scribner's (juvenile novel, serialized 1951)
THE GREEN HILLS OF EARTH	Shasta (collection: Delilah and the Space-Rigger, 1949; Space Jockey, 1947; The Long Watch, 1949; Gentlemen, Be Seated, 1948; The Black Pits of Luna, 1948; "It's Great to Be Back!," 1947; "—We Also Walk Dogs," 1941; Ordeal in Space, 1948; The Green Hills of Earth, 1947; Logic of Empire, 1941)
THE PUPPET MASTERS	Doubleday (novel, serialized 1951)
TOMORROW, THE STARS	Doubleday (anthology, edited by Robert A. Heinlein)
UNIVERSE	Dell (paperback edition of 1941 story)

1952

The Year of the Jackpot	*Galaxy Science Fiction*, March 1952
Tramp Space Ship (The Rolling Stones)	*Boys' Life*, Sept., Oct., Nov., Dec. 1952
THE ROLLING STONES	Scribner's (juvenile novel, serialized 1952)

1953

Project Nightmare	*Amazing Stories*, April 1953
Sky Lift	*Imagination*, Nov. 1953
ASSIGNMENT IN ETERNITY	Fantasy Press (collection: Gulf, 1949; Elsewhen, 1941; Lost Legacy, 1941; Jerry Was a Man, 1947)
REVOLT IN 2100	Shasta (collection: "If This Goes On—," 1940; Coventry, 1940; Misfit, 1939)
STARMAN JONES	Scribner's (original juvenile novel)

1954

Star Lummox (The Star Beast)	*Fantasy and Science Fiction*, May, June, July 1954
THE STAR BEAST	Scribner's (juvenile novel, serialized 1954)

1955

TUNNEL IN THE SKY	Scribner's (original juvenile novel)

1956

Double Star	*Astounding Science Fiction*, Feb., March, April 1956
The Door Into Summer	*Fantasy and Science Fiction*, Oct., Nov., Dec. 1956
DOUBLE STAR	Doubleday (novel, serialized 1956)
TIME FOR THE STARS	Scribner's (original juvenile novel)

1957

The Menace from Earth	*Fantasy and Science Fiction*, Aug. 1957
Citizen of the Galaxy	*Astounding Science Fiction*, Sept., Oct., Nov., Dec. 1957
The Elephant Circuit (The Man Who Traveled in Elephants)	*Saturn*, Oct. 1957
CITIZEN OF THE GALAXY	Scribner's (juvenile novel, serialized 1957)
THE DOOR INTO SUMMER	Doubleday (novel, serialized 1956)

1958

Tenderfoot in Space	*Boys' Life*, May, June, July 1958
Have Space Suit—Will Travel	*Fantasy and Science Fiction*, Aug., Sept., Oct. 1958
HAVE SPACE SUIT— WILL TRAVEL	Scribner's (juvenile novel, serialized 1958)
METHUSELAH'S CHILDREN	Gnome Press (novel, serialized 1941)

1959

"All You Zombies—"   *Fantasy and Science Fiction*, March 1959
Starship Soldier   *Fantasy and Science Fiction*, Oct., Nov.,
(Starship Troopers)   1959
THE MENACE FROM EARTH   Gnome Press (collection: The Year of the
                                  Jackpot, 1952; By His Bootstraps, 1941;
                                  Columbus Was a Dope, 1947; The Men-
                                  ace from Earth, 1957; Sky Lift, 1953;
                                  Goldfish Bowl, 1942; Project Night-
                                  mare, 1953; Water Is for Washing, 1947)
STARSHIP TROOPERS   Putnam (juvenile novel, serialized 1959)
THE UNPLEASANT PROFESSION
   OF JONATHAN HOAG   Gnome Press (collection: The Unpleasant
                                  Profession of Jonathan Hoag, 1942;
                                  The Man Who Traveled in Elephants,
                                  1957; "All You Zombies—," 1959;
                                  They, 1941; Our Fair City, 1948; "And
                                  He Built a Crooked House," 1940)

1960

no fiction published

1961

STRANGER IN A STRANGE
   LAND   Putnam (original novel)

1962

Searchlight   *Scientific American*, Aug. 1962, and other
                                  magazines (advertisement)
Podkayne of Mars   *If*, Nov. 1962, Jan., March 1963

1963

Glory Road   *Fantasy and Science Fiction*, July, Aug.,
                                  Sept. 1963
GLORY ROAD   Putnam (novel, serialized 1963)
PODKAYNE OF MARS   Putnam (juvenile novel, serialized 1962-3)

1964

Farnham's Freehold   *If*, July, Sept., Oct. 1964
FARNHAM'S FREEHOLD   Putnam (novel, serialized 1964)
ORPHANS OF THE SKY   Putnam (collection: Universe, 1941; Com-
                                  mon Sense, 1941)

The Moon Is a Harsh Mistress
THREE BY HEINLEIN

Free Men

THE MOON IS A HARSH
  MISTRESS
THE WORLDS OF ROBERT
  A. HEINLEIN

THE PAST THROUGH
  TOMORROW

1965

If, Dec. 1965, Jan., Feb., Mar., Apr. 1966
Doubleday (omnibus: The Puppet Masters,
  1951; Waldo, 1942; Magic, Inc., 1940)

1966

(original short story in THE WORLDS
  OF ROBERT A. HEINLEIN)

Putnam (novel, serialized 1965-6)

Ace Books (paperback collection: Free
  Men, 1966; Blowups Happen, 1940;
  Searchlight, 1962; Life-Line, 1939;
  Solution Unsatisfactory, 1940)

1967

Putnam (the Future History, revised and
  nearly complete: Life-Line, 1939; The
  Roads Must Roll, 1940; Blowups Hap-
  pen, 1940; The Man Who Sold the
  Moon, 1950; Delilah and the Space-
  Rigger, 1949; Space Jockey, 1947; Re-
  quiem, 1940; The Long Watch, 1949;
  Gentlemen, Be Seated, 1948; The Black
  Pits of Luna, 1948; "It's Great to Be
  Back!," 1947; "—We Also Walk Dogs,"
  1941; Searchlight, 1962; Ordeal in
  Space, 1948; The Green Hills of Earth,
  1947; Logic of Empire, 1941; The Men-
  ace from Earth, 1957; "If This Goes
  On—," 1940; Coventry, 1940; Misfit,
  1939; Methuselah's Children, 1941)